HEAVY EQUIPMENT

MICHAEL ALVES, KEITH HADDOCK,
HANS HALBERSTADT and SAM SARGENT

CRESTLINE

CRESTLINE

An imprint of MBI Publishing Company

The edition published in 2003 by Crestline, an imprint of MBI Publishing Company, Galtier Plaza, Suite 200, 380 Jackson Street, St. Paul, MN 55101-3885 USA

First published by MBI Publishing Company.

Colossal Earthmovers © Keith Haddock, 2000
Giant Dump Trucks © Hans Halberstadt, 1994
Bulldozers © Sam Sargent and Michael Alves, 1994

Motorbooks International titles are also available at discounts in bulk quantity for industrial or sales-promotional use. For details write to Special Sales Manager at Motorbooks International Wholesalers & Distributors, Galtier Plaza, Suite 200, 380 Jackson Street, St. Paul, MN 55101-3885 USA.

ISBN 0-7603-1775-5

Front cover: A mighty Caterpillar D10N pushes a mass of dirt in the course of a day's work.

Front banner (left to right): There are quiet accomodations for two in the spacious air conditioned cab of the Dresser Haulpak truck.

The Marion 6360 was the largest stripping shovel of its kind.

A Komatsu bulldozer cuts a quarry terrace.

The Caterpillar 797 debuted in 1998, 50 percent larger than Caterpillar's previous largest machine.

On the title page: This Bucyrus-Erie 1950-B was christened the Silver Spade and was the first of two built by Bucyrus-Erie Company for the Hanna Coal Company.

On the back cover: The ore is nicely pulverized by the application of explosives, making it easy for the shovel to scoop it up and deposit it aboard this WISEDA truck.

Contents

COLOSSAL EARTHMOVERS

GIANT DUMP TRUCKS

BULLDOZERS

Colossal Earthmovers

Keith Haddock

ACKNOWLEDGMENTS

I would like to give special thanks to the many individuals and organizations who have helped to make this publication not just another picture book, but a book filled with accurate data and spectacular images of the colossal machines of the earthmoving world. The people listed below, and others too numerous to mention, have supported me in my endeavors. I really appreciate your time and efforts. A special thanks to my friend and author Eric Orlemann for providing many of his superb images.

Aidan Mitchell, Krupp Canada; Alvin E. Nus, Volvo Construction Equipment; Bill Williams, P&H Mining Equipment; Bob Jelinek, Bucyrus International, Inc.; Bob Pierce, Unit Rig, Div. Terex; Bruce Knight, Transwest Dynequip; Darin McCoy, CMI Corporation; Dave Lang, Bucyrus International, Inc.; Dave Sharples, Komatsu America International Co.; Dave Wootton, Hednesford, England; Debbie Campbell, Terex Construction Equipment, Scotland; Denis Gaspe, Fording Coal Ltd.; Dimitrie Toth Jr., Waterford, Michigan, U.S.A.; Don Frantz, Historical Construction Equipment Association; Edward Kress, Kress Corporation; Eric Orlemann, ECO Communications; Francis Pierre, ATM, Malakoff, France; G.W. von Alten, O&K Div. Terex, Germany; Gordon Morris, Wajax Industries Ltd.; Hal Lundeen, Terex Mining, Canada; Ian Hamilton, Terex Equipment Ltd., Scotland; Jim Rosso, Bucyrus International, Inc.; John Leach, Hitachi Construction Machinery Canada Ltd.; Lee Haak, Komatsu America International Co.; Mark Sprouls, Schaumburg, Illinois, U.S.A.; Merilee Hunt, Liebherr Mining Equipment Co.; Michael VonFlattern, Innovative Mining & Equipment, Inc.; Mike Holland, Holland Construction Co.; Pete Holman, Caterpillar, Inc.; Peter Ahrenkiel, Terex Mining, U.S.A.; Peter Gilewicz, Parker Bay Company; Peter Grimshaw, PNG Communications, England; Peter Winkel, Liebherr France; Stuart Davis, Rimpull Corporation; Tim Backus, P&H Mining Equipment; Tom Berry, Historical Construction Equipment Association; Ulrich Wulfert, Demag Komatsu GmbH, Germany; Yvon LeCadre, Trignac, France. Last but not least, a special thanks to my dear wife Barbara, who meticulously edited this text and continues to support me in my writing endeavors.

INTRODUCTION

Welcome to the world of colossal earthmovers, the largest machines and vehicles ever to move on land. The detailed text and photographs in this book provide a spectacular look at the largest of each type of earthmoving machine. These machines must be big because of the immense tasks they perform. They are designed to move vast quantities of earth to uncover valuable minerals—a daunting task that has stretched human ingenuity to its limits in order to build the largest machines possible.

The machines described and illustrated in this book are usually found in surface mining operations or sometimes on large construction projects. Their owners demand the lowest unit cost of material moved, and the shortest payback time for the huge initial purchase cost. Therefore, manufacturers must make these machines large enough to minimize cost per cubic yard moved, and reliable and efficient enough to work for many years.

Viewed from a distance, these super-sized machines appear insignificant. Their immensity only becomes apparent when observed at close range, or when a person or familiar object appears in the picture. These machines are so large that they must be taken apart into transportable pieces when moving from job to job, and some might take over a year to erect.

Since 1835 when the first machine to move earth was introduced, earthmoving machines have been tremendous benefits to mankind, and essential contributors to the modern lifestyle we now enjoy. These machines built railroads to open up vast uncharted territories, built canals to shorten shipping routes, and reclaimed millions of acres of land from swamps by constructing levees to drain low-lying land.

Extensive fleets of bulldozers, scrapers, shovels, and haulers built roads for the automobile age, including one of the greatest projects in U.S. history: the interstate highway system. Since 1956, 42,800 miles of interstate highway have been constructed.

The surface mining industry necessitated the creation of the very largest earthmoving machines. The vast open-pit mines used for the extraction of valuable minerals, such as copper and gold, constantly demand larger machines. Annual production of coal, over half coming from surface mines, is increasing each year as electric power generation companies increase their capacity.

Unlike the early days of strip mining when reclamation (replacing the earth) was not carried out, today's efficient machines can recover vast tonnages of valuable minerals from a site, and then reclaim it to such a degree that it becomes hard to tell where the mine existed. Today the public is more than willing to pay the extra cost of reclamation in order to protect the environment.

Selecting the small number of photographs specified for this book from the many hundreds of suitable photographs was a difficult task. The author hopes that readers familiar with the machines will appreciate the images selected, and that readers who are less familiar with the machines will gain an insight to the fascinating world of heavy equipment. The text was taken from the author's historical archives and is the result of more than 25 years of collecting data, photographs, and literature. Every effort has been made to deliver the most accurate information, most of which was obtained from the manufacturers' own records. *Colossal Earthmovers* is a perfect companion to the author's previous book, *Giant Earthmovers: An Illustrated History*, which is a historical reference book on the subject of earthmoving equipment.

11

Chapter 1

BULLDOZERS

Modern civilization is largely a product of earthmoving machines. Of all the different types of earthmoving machines, the bulldozer is the most frequently used on construction projects today. From the quarrying of building materials and the mining of precious metals and coal, to the construction of roads, houses, and factories, bulldozers can be seen doing a multitude of tasks on every project.

Basically, the bulldozer pushes dirt around. That sounds like an easy thing to do, but let's look at the work more closely. Access roads have to be constructed and maintained. Holes have to be dug and filled in. Dump areas have to be leveled. Other vehicles have to be pulled or pushed out when stuck. Gravel has to be spread. Then, when the job is nearly finished, the bulldozer is assigned to the final landscaping and reclamation. This usually includes a layer of topsoil neatly spread over the site prior to seeding. All these tasks are performed expertly by the bulldozer.

The most powerful bulldozer currently in production is the Komatsu D575A-2 Super Dozer. At 1,150 horsepower and a 157-ton weight, this colossal machine is used to reclaim surface mines. *Komatsu Mining Systems*

The bulldozer is simple. It's a powerful tractor with good traction and a power-controlled dozer blade mounted in front. But that's not the whole story. The tractor must be built of tough, reliable components and designed to the highest standards that technology can provide. That's because bulldozers operate in some of the most rigorous and demanding conditions experienced by any machine. From tough rock-ripping assignments to being submerged over its tracks in mud, from subzero temperatures to desert heat, the bulldozer must push through. Modern operators cannot tolerate frequent breakdowns, so bulldozers must be dependable day after day, night after night.

The first bulldozers were wooden blades pushed by a pair of horses. The giant machines of today evolved from early crawler tractors designed for agriculture. First developed by the Holt Manufacturing Company beginning in 1904, the crawler tractor soon found use in construction applications. As crawler tractors became more robust and reliable, they were found to be ideal for carrying a bulldozer blade. The early tractor-mounted blades, however, did not have power control. It was left to the operator (or an assistant) to crank the blade up and down by means of

The Caterpillar Diesel Thirty Five tractor was introduced in 1933 with 41 drawbar horsepower. This example is equipped with bolt-on grouser pads, so that it can operate on streets without tearing up the pavement. The Caterpillar pull-type grader behind this tractor is a type of machine that was popular up to the 1950s, until it was made obsolete by more efficient motor graders. *Keith Haddock*

tiresome, wrist-wrenching hand wheels. Cable-operated blades worked by winches soon superseded these, and as early as 1925, hydraulically operated blades began to appear.

One of the most significant pre–World War II bulldozers was Caterpillar's Diesel Seventy-Five, 83-horsepower tractor coming out in 1933. This model grew into the first Caterpillar D8, the 1H series, in 1935. As they say, the rest is history. More than 60 years later, the D8 is still being produced, having progressed through its suffix letters to the present D8R model. The D8 was joined by the famous D9 in 1955, which also progressed through many model changes to the present D9R model.

Bulldozers by the thousand helped to win World War II. Bulldozer blades, mostly built by the R. G. LeTourneau Company, were mounted on crawler tractors and made their way overseas or to Alaska to prepare the ground for fighting forces. Admiral William F. Halsey stated, "The four machines that won the war in the Pacific were the submarine, radar, the airplane and the bulldozer."

By the mid-1950s bulldozers were no longer a tractor with an attachment. They were an integrated unit, designed for production from the ground up. Bulldozers from the major manufacturers could be seen with equal frequency on the big jobs, and the manufacturers competed with each other to produce the biggest machine. The "big red teams" of International TD-24s, and the fleets of Persian orange Allis-Chalmers HD-21s, ran side by side with the latest bright yellow Caterpillar models, including the just-launched D9s. Then the Euclid green TC-12, the largest crawler tractor in the world, gave the long-time tractor makers more competition when it hit the dirt in 1955.

These 1950s giants were impressive, but they pale in comparison to today's colossal tractors. Spearheaded by Caterpillar's "high-drive" D10 in the 1970s, the push for larger tractors has continued to the current largest: Komatsu's D575A-2, boasting almost three times the power of the largest crawler built in the 1950s.

Because the demand for large bulldozers exceeded the capability of state-of-the-art engines and transmissions in the 1960s, a transitional phase took place before the super dozer era in

which the largest tractors were doubled-up and run by one operator. Typical of these was Caterpillar's SxS D9G (two tractors side by side with 24-foot dozer blade). The two-tractor concept survived until 1978, when it was eclipsed by the introduction of Caterpillar's D10.

Caterpillar's first "high-drive" tractor, the D10, was a major breakthrough for the industry. The main advantages of placing the track drive sprocket high above the ground are that a cushioned undercarriage instead of the drive axle absorbs uneven ground shocks, and the drivetrain is kept out of the mud. High drive is now standard on all Caterpillar's medium and large crawler tractors, which include the company's largest, the 840-horsepower D11R. On one version of this tractor, Caterpillar mounts its largest dozer blade and calls it the

The Euclid TC-12 was the world's most powerful tractor when it came out in 1955. Sporting two engines mounted on each side of a split frame, the 402-horsepower monster is steered by adjusting the speed and direction of each engine transmission. *Eric C. Orlemann collection*

Used for reclaiming surface mines, this 24-foot blade is pushed by two Caterpillar D9H tractors hooked together to form an 820-horsepower unit controlled by one operator. *Eric C. Orlemann*

D11R CD (Carry-Dozer). This has a special, 22-foot-wide curved blade, enabling it to carry more material than a standard blade.

Allis-Chalmers built some of the world's largest crawler tractors and bulldozers during its long history. From its diesel-powered tractor line in 1940, the HD-14 at 108 horsepower was the most powerful crawler tractor available at that time. In 1947, Allis-Chalmers again broke the crawler tractor size record with the introduction of the 163-horsepower HD-19 with torque converter drive. In 1970 another world-record beater, the massive HD-41 with an operating weight of 70 tons and 524-horsepower engine, was introduced. From 1974 Allis-Chalmers construction machines were known as Fiat-Allis following a joint venture set up by Fiat. In 1989, manufacture was discontinued in North America, but Fiat-Allis machines are still imported from Italy.

International Harvester was also known for big tractors in the 1950s and 1960s. The company launched its TD-24 in 1947, claiming to be the world's largest crawler tractor. At 180 horsepower, it clipped the title from the Allis-Chalmers HD-19, which came out earlier the same year. The TD-24 and its updates remained in production until 1959 and were seen on many of the biggest earthmoving jobs of the 1950s. An even larger tractor, the TD-30, was introduced in 1962. This heavyweight 320-horsepower tractor competed with Caterpillar's D9, but only remained in production for some five years.

The largest-ever International crawler tractor was developed in the early 1980s and launched in 1985 as the Dresser TD-40. International's crawler line had been bought by Dresser Industries Inc. three years earlier. Initially built in the United States, the TD-40

This is the Carry Dozer (CD) version of Caterpillar's largest bulldozer, the D11R. Developing 840 horsepower, the D11R CD can push and carry enough material with its 22-foot blade to fill an average-size living room. *Keith Haddock*

weighed more than 67 tons with a dozer blade and ran with a 460-horsepower Cummins engine. This tractor has since been upgraded to the present 520-horsepower Dresser TD-40C now built in Poland. Today the machines are sold under Komatsu America International Company.

As early as 1981, Japan's Komatsu broke the 1,000-horsepower threshold with its 133-ton D555A at the Conexpo exhibition in Houston, Texas, and today Komatsu can boast the largest production model bulldozer—the D575A-2 SD. It uses a whopping 1,150 horsepower to push its 24-foot-wide dozer blade. This 157-ton machine was introduced in 1995.

Another large bulldozer, the Model T-50.01, is built today in the former Soviet Union. This is a 750-horsepower machine with an operating weight of just over than 100 tons.

In the 1980s, Italian contractor Umberto ACCO built the largest crawler tractor of all time for an earthmoving contract in Libya. With two engines mounted side by side under the hood and a total of 1,300 horsepower, the giant dozer is two stories high, and measures almost 40 feet from blade to ripper. Equipped with Caterpillar engines and transmissions, the machine weighs 183 tons.

Rubber-tired tractors fitted with dozer blades or push blocks are known as wheel dozers and represent some of the largest bulldozer-type machines ever constructed. They are used as clean-up machines under large shovels, to stockpile coal and other minerals, for heavy bulldozing such as reclamation work, or in push-loading scrapers. They are especially popular in large surface mines where their high-speed mobility is essential for traveling between different assignments.

R. G. LeTourneau Inc., famous for its innovative equipment, started building huge wheel dozers in 1947. The first series were mechanically driven. They were steered using the "skid steer" principle. Steering is accomplished by locking the wheels on one side of the vehicle while the other side remains in motion, allowing the vehicle to turn. The most popular was the Model C Tournadozer. By the mid-1950s, LeTourneau dozers were electrically driven with motors in each wheel. The dozers got bigger in the 1960s with the introduction of the K-series monsters. The largest was the K-205 fitted with three 420-horsepower Cummins engines and weighing in at 160 tons.

International's largest wheel dozer happened to be the first they ever built. That was back in 1961 when the 600-horsepower D-500 was unveiled. This 64-ton machine was claimed to be the world's first articulated wheel dozer. From this machine, International developed its large articulated wheel loaders.

Caterpillar's first wheel dozers, appearing in 1963, were the 824 and 834 of 300 and 400 horsepower. Since then the line has been expanded and upgraded. In 1997, Caterpillar further boosted its wheel dozer line by purchasing the manufacturing rights to two dozers from Tiger Engineering Ltd. of Australia. The two models are now the 844 and 854G and represent Caterpillar's largest wheel dozers ranging up to 800 horsepower.

In 1970, CF & I Engineers of Denver, Colorado, came out with an eight-wheel rigid-frame dozer equipped with two 335-horsepower engines. Since the wheels on each side of the

The most powerful and heaviest crawler bulldozer of all time was the Italian ACCO. Only one was ever made and that was in 1980. Both the upper and lower rear sprockets drove the tracks, with power coming from two engines, totaling 1,300 horsepower. *Yvon LeCadre*

This K600A was one of a series of large wheel dozers equipped with diesel-electric drive that were made by LeTourneau in the 1960s. The 635-horsepower unit (shown here) is helping to load a Terex scraper at Cape Coral, Florida. *Eric C. Orlemann collection*

Ready for action is this LeTourneau D-800 dozer of 800 horsepower. The LeTourneau D-series dozers and L-series loaders are derived from the same diesel-electric tractors. *Keith Haddock*

When International Harvester unveiled the D-500 dozer in 1961, it claimed to be the first articulated-frame wheel dozer. At 600 horsepower, it was the largest dozer ever built by International. *Keith Haddock*

machine were driven by their own engine, steering was accomplished using skid steer. Manufacture of this 70-ton machine was taken over by Melroe of Bobcat Loader fame in the mid-1970s. Since 1996, the machine has been available from Innovative Mining and Equipment of Gillette, Wyoming, and its power has been boosted to 850 horsepower.

Another large wheel dozer was the V-Con Dozer designed by the Peerless Manufacturing Company of Dallas, Texas. This 1,500-horse-power diesel-electric machine with wheel motors in each wheel was designed for reclamation at surface mines. In 1973, the Marion Power Shovel Company took over the marketing of the V-Con.

The largest wheel dozer ever built roamed the earth more than 35 years ago when this one-of-a-kind machine was built for Western Contracting Corporation in 1963. First used

This monster is one of the largest bulldozers ever built. Known as the V-Con V220, it carries a diesel-electric power unit of 1,500 horsepower and uses electric motors in each wheel. Marion Power Shovel Company marketed the V-Con for a few years in the mid-1970s. *Eric C. Orlemann collection*

on the 17-million-yard Milford Dam job in Kansas, the 1,850-horsepower diesel-electric outfit still claims to be the most powerful wheel or crawler dozer of all time. With an electric motor in each of its four wheels, both ends of this 47-foot-long behemoth were articulated, providing the unit with a tidy 37 1/2-foot turning radius. This special machine was a great success for Western Contracting Corporation, which kept it working until 1981.

The Melroe M870 steers by the skid-steer principle. Chains drive the tires on each side. This giant machine uses its two 335-horsepower engines to push its three-way tilting blade. *Innovative Mining and Equipment Inc.*

Chapter 2

WHEEL LOADERS

The wheel loader originated in the 1920s when small agricultural-type tractors were fitted with a loader bucket. Primarily designed as a rehandling shovel for light materials, the loader has gradually developed into a heavier machine for earthmoving applications. Because of its greater capabilities and superior mobility, the wheel loader has not only become one of the most popular machines seen on construction sites, it has also expanded its usefulness into sand and gravel pits and surface mining. With the exception of the large electric mining shovels, loaders have largely taken over the work previously done by the crawler-mounted cable shovels popular in the 1950s. And in surface mines, today's largest loaders now perform duties always thought to be the exclusive domain of the cable excavator.

The earliest wheel loaders were cable-operated. The bucket was hoisted through a clutch-operated winch, then dumped by grav-

ity through a trip-release mechanism. By the late 1930s, the first integrated machines began to appear. These were machines built specifically as a loader rather than a tractor with an attachment. After World War II, established manufacturers began to produce wheel loaders in larger sizes, and several new manufacturers joined the competition. Hydraulic systems were proven on loaders in the 1940s, making the cable types obsolete by the end of the decade.

A significant step in the development of the wheel loader was the introduction of the articulated frame. Mixermobile Manufacturers of Portland, Oregon, pioneered this concept in 1953 with its Scoopmobile Model LD-5. Like so many other brilliant innovations, articulation was slow to be appreciated. Eventually its greater maneuverability and resulting shorter cycle time was recognized by the entire loader industry. The leading makers began introducing articulated models into their lines: Caterpillar in 1963, International Hough in 1964, Michigan and Allis-Chalmers in 1965, and Trojan in 1966. Today all large wheel loaders, and most of the small units, have an articulated frame.

Throughout the 1960s the trend was to build ever larger wheel loaders. Industry surveys in 1963 showed a need for loaders much

---

The massive LeTourneau L-1800 is the world's largest wheel loader. Available with buckets from 28 to 55 cubic yards, it rides on four 12-foot-diameter tires. The one shown here is loading coal at Peabody Coal's Rochelle Mine, Wyoming. *Eric C. Orlemann*

Caterpillar's 994 is the company's top-of-the-line wheel loader as of 1999. The 23-yard bucket is dwarfed by the huge tires measuring 12 feet in diameter. The colossal 196-ton machine receives a brief inspection before returning to rock-loading duties. *Eric C. Orlemann*

bigger than the 5- to 6-cubic-yard standard machines then available. The Hough Division of International Harvester responded with its 10-cubic-yard H-400 in 1964 derived from its D-500 wheel dozer. Other loaders in the 10-yard class soon followed—the Michigan 475 in 1965, the Scoopmobile 1200 in 1967, and the Caterpillar 992 in 1968.

The established tractor builder Caterpillar entered the wheel loader market with its 2-cubic-yard Model 944 in 1959. Four years later the 6-yard Model 988 was introduced as Caterpillar's largest loader up to that time, and its first articulated loader. Another big jump in size was achieved in 1968 with the introduction of the 10-yard 992. The 992B followed in 1973, and then a further jump in size occurred in 1977 when the 12 1/2-yard 992C with a 690 flywheel horsepower engine was launched.

Caterpillar's flagship loader today is the giant 994D, one of the biggest loaders currently in the field. First available in 1991 as the 994, the D model has a standard bucket of 23 cubic yards and an operating weight of 211 tons. It is powered by a single Caterpillar 3516 engine with 1,250 flywheel horsepower. Large loaders, such as the 994, are valuable in large open pit mines where they can take over from a large electric shovel that may be down for maintenance. The large loaders can move quickly from point to point in the mine and are capable of loading the largest trucks. They run on tires up to 13 feet in diameter, some of the largest ever made.

The first integrated four-wheel-drive loader from Case was the W-9 loader introduced

This International 580 Payloader was one of three used to remove overburden at Andalex Resources' coal mine in Kentucky. At 22-cubic-yards capacity and 1,075 flywheel horsepower, the 580 was the largest International loader before Dresser bought the line in 1982. *Keith Haddock*

in 1958. Further loaders in the W-series followed throughout the 1960s and 1970s reaching 4 cubic yards with the Model W36. Beginning in 1987, the entire Case loader line graduated into the 21-series. The largest of these is the current Model 921C, which carries a 4 3/4-cubic-yard standard bucket.

John Deere is the most recent of the "big name" construction equipment manufacturers to enter into four-wheel-drive wheel loader production. The company chose 1967 to launch the first of its wheel loader line, the JD-544. The articulated, four-wheel-drive machine came out with a 94-horsepower engine and buckets up to 3 cubic yards. John Deere's biggest loader, the 844, appeared in 1979, featuring a newly developed V-8 John Deere diesel engine.

Dart, a famous off-highway truck builder, launched a large loader in 1966. The huge mechanical-drive D600, with its isolated cab overhanging one side, had a distinctive ap-

pearance and boasted a 15-cubic-yard capacity, the largest production loader then available. The standard engine offered was a Cummins VT12 at 700 maximum horsepower. The D600 and its subsequent upgrades, the D600B and 600C, proved very popular with mining and earthmoving contractors. Many hundreds were sold from its introduction to the last in 1995.

In 1971, International Harvester announced the world's biggest wheel loader at the American Mining Congress in Las Vegas. This was the H-580 Payloader carrying an 18-cubic-yard standard rock bucket. It was almost double the size of the company's previous largest Payloader, the H-400B. International Payloaders had their origins in the Frank G. Hough Company, which built wheel loaders from 1939. Other significant Hough "firsts" were the first hydraulically actuated bucket tilt in 1944 and the world's first four-wheel-drive, hydraulically operated loader in 1947. International merged with Hough in 1952.

In 1982, Dresser Industries acquired International Harvester's Payline Division, and the trade name *Dresser* was adopted for the loaders. Yet another change took place in 1988 when Japan's Komatsu Ltd. and Dresser Industries Inc. formed the Komatsu Dresser Company (KDC) to market both companies' lines. The top-of-the-line 580 Payloader, already upgraded to 22-yard capacity by 1975, grew into the massive 24-yard Haulpak 4000 by 1992, but it was discontinued in 1996. The current top-of-the-line Komatsu loader is the WA-1200 introduced at the end of 1999. It boasts a standard bucket of 26 cubic yards and develops 1,560 horsepower.

In keeping with its long tradition of record-breaking machines, today's LeTourneau line includes the largest wheel loaders ever built. Still made in the Longview, Texas, plant established by its founder, R. G. LeTourneau, the loader line spans bucket sizes from 17 to 45 cubic yards. The top-of-the-line L-1800 wields a standard bucket of 33 cubic yards, and it can carry buckets up to 45 yards for coal loading. Used in surface mining for coal loading or overburden removal, the behemoth L-1800 rides on four 12-foot-diameter tires, the largest in the industry.

LeTourneau loaders feature diesel-electric drive with DC electric motors in each wheel, a design configuration R. G. LeTourneau developed many years earlier. LeTourneau produced some gigantic electric loaders in the early 1960s, with power to the hoist and bucket tilt transmitted through a rack-and-pinion drive. One example was the Model SL-10 with a bucket of 10 cubic yards, an unheard-of size when introduced in 1960. By 1965 the record-beating SL-40 was launched. Nicknamed the Monster, it sported a 19-yard rock bucket and twin GM engines, totaling 950 horsepower. Some of these rack-and-pinion loaders had a working life of more than 20 years.

In 1953, Clark Equipment Company began its Construction Machinery Division at Benton Harbor, Michigan. A year later, Michigan introduced three wheel loaders, the forerunners of a line of loaders that would include the world's largest by the 1970s.

It was big news in the industry when Michigan announced its giant 675 loader.

The WA1200 Mountain Mover is the latest and largest loader from Komatsu Mining Systems. Powered by a 1,560 horsepower Cummins engine, this colossal machine carries a standard rock bucket of 26.2 cubic yards. *Komatsu Mining Systems*

LeTourneau builds the world's biggest wheel loaders. Here is an early version, a 1965 Model SL-40 with a 19-yard bucket. Typical of LeTourneau machines of the era, this loader features rack-and-pinion steering and bucket movements. *Eric C. Orlemann collection*

Twice as big as Michigan's previous largest Model 475 loader, it was also the largest wheel loader ever built up to that time. The prototype was built in 1970 and was powered by two GM engines. Then from 1973 to 1976, a further 14 production models were built with twin Cummins engines totaling 1,270 horsepower. The operator sat in a cab two stories above the ground and rode on four tires more than 10 feet in diameter, the largest in the industry.

Clark Michigan Company became a subsidiary of VME Group N.V. in 1985, and the Michigan line gradually merged into Volvo's own line of wheel loaders. By 1994 the Michigan name disappeared in favor of the Volvo name.

This LeTourneau L-1200 is on show at the company's Longview, Texas, proving ground in 1981. It carries a bucket of 22 cubic yards and a 1,200-horsepower diesel engine. *Keith Haddock*

The Michigan 675 was a monster for its day. Sporting two engines totaling 1,270 horsepower and a 24-yard bucket, it was in production from 1973 to 1976. The tires are 10 feet in diameter. *Volvo Construction Machinery*

Chapter 3

SCRAPERS

Scrapers are the big digging and hauling machines seen on many highway and construction jobs. The larger self-propelled types, running on giant rubber tires, are capable of moving vast quantities of earth at high speed. Scrapers are versatile. They can load, haul, and dump—all in one operating cycle. But most of them are not designed to load themselves, and they usually require assistance from a push tractor to load. There are a few true self-loading types known as elevating or auger scrapers, and these are fitted with a powered elevator or auger to help raise the earth into the scraper bowl.

Scrapers evolved from a simple box drawn by horses and date back to the time when man first used animals to undertake strenuous tasks. When steam traction engines came on the scene in the late 19th century, scrapers were often towed behind them to grade earth for road construction and for drainage in agriculture.

Typical of the monster scrapers built by LeTourneau in the mid-1960s is this Model 6-30 Electric Digger. It featured telescoping scraper bowls and could self-load 180 tons of earth. Only one was built and that for experimental purposes. *Eric C. Orlemann collection*

With the advent of the crawler tractor, scrapers became a recognized way of moving earth when towed behind this new form of motive power. In fact, the tractor-scraper outfit was the perfect tool for road construction where cuts and fills required material to be moved relatively short distances.

The forerunners of today's high-speed earthmovers appeared in the late 1930s when self-propelled scrapers were pioneered by R. G. LeTourneau. The earliest motor scraper was the Model A Tournapull. It ran on large rubber tires, a first in the industry. It also had a revolutionary two-wheel tractor design, enabling the tractor to swing 90 degrees in each direction. This huge machine could carry enough dirt to fill an average living room at speeds up to 20 miles per hour. The basic design of the first Tournapull still exists in scrapers to the present day.

Initially slow to catch on, motor scrapers gradually gained in popularity spurred on by the earthmoving demands of World War II and massive construction projects such as the interstate system in the 1950s. Continuing into the 1960s, scrapers were found in large fleets as primary earthmoving tools in surface mining and dam construction. The 1960s also saw the largest scrapers ever built.

The pioneer of the motor scraper, R. G. LeTourneau, also built the world's largest scrapers in its Electric Digger series, the first of which appeared at the American Mining Congress in 1958. Known as the Goliath, or Model A4, it was the largest self-propelled scraper to date, and like all subsequent LeTourneau scrapers, featured electric motors in every wheel. It also incorporated the familiar LeTourneau feature of rack and pinion for steering and scraper operation.

Although a large number of types and sizes were built, the Electric Diggers never sold in large quantities. In fact most of them were classed as "experimental" and did not pass the prototype stage. The huge tandem and triple-bowl outfits with multiple engines were the most famous of all. The LT-360 Electric Digger with three bowls was the biggest scraper ever built and had a combined capacity of 216 cubic yards. It moved on eight wheels measuring more than 10 feet in diameter and was powered with eight engines of 635 horsepower each! It was the largest earthmover ever mounted on rubber tires.

The forerunner of the present-day Caterpillar line of motor scrapers made its debut in 1951. It was the DW-21, and it featured

One of the most popular Caterpillar 600-series scrapers is the 631 shown here in its modern "E" format. It has a heaped capacity of 31 cubic yards. *Keith Haddock*

The Model 666 was the biggest scraper Caterpillar ever produced. The twin-powered machine had a total of 980 horsepower and a heaped rating of 54 cubic yards. It continued in production as the 666B until 1978. *Caterpillar Inc.*

Caterpillar's first two-wheel tractor unit coupled to a cable-operated scraper of 18-cubic-yards heaped capacity. Other DW-series scrapers of smaller capacity followed during the 1950s. Then, beginning in 1960, Caterpillar introduced the first of its 600 series motor scrapers, the 619, with 18-cubic-yard heaped capacity. By 1962, a full line of 600 series scrapers was available with capacities ranging up to 54 heaped yards in the Model 666. This twin-engine scraper with a four-wheel tractor had a combined power rating of 980 horsepower. Uprated to the 666B in 1969, it remained in Caterpillar's line until 1978. The 666 is still the largest scraper ever built by Caterpillar.

Along with LeTourneau, Euclid was the other company to pioneer the high-speed earthmoving capabilities of self-propelled scrapers. Euclid's prototype scraper, known as the 1SH, was in the field as early as 1938 and was the forerunner of Euclid's extensive scraper line developed over the next three decades. These scrapers included overhung (two-wheel tractor) and four-wheel tractor types. Euclid's first twin scraper, with engines at front and rear, came out in 1949 initially rated at 16 cubic yards struck capacity, but was later uprated to 18 yards. In 1957, Euclid launched what would become one of the most famous large scrapers of all time—the twin-powered TS-24 with 24-cubic-yards

struck capacity. It is still in production today as the Terex TS-24C.

The huge 40-cubic-yard TSS-40, with four-wheel tractor and powered by two GM engines developing 810 gross horsepower, rolled on the scene in 1963. Not content with these largest scrapers available at the time, famous earthmoving contractor Western Contracting Corporation ordered a fleet of Euclid TTSS-40 scraper units in 1964. These huge outfits had three GM engines, and the combination of two bowls provided a struck capacity of more than 80 cubic yards. These were the largest scrapers Euclid ever built. Euclid was a division of General Motors Corporation (GM) from 1953, but in 1968 GM's earthmoving products became known by the name Terex.

Michigan entered the scraper market in 1957 after a short development period. Their scrapers were a product of the Construction

A large fleet of these biggest-ever Euclid scrapers was ordered for the Castaic Dam job in California by Western Contracting Corporation in 1964. They were Tandem TSS-40 scrapers powered by three GM 16V-71 engines. Each bowl had a capacity of 40 cubic yards (struck). *Eric C. Orlemann collection*

Machinery Division set up by Clark Equipment Company in 1952. Clark management decided the company would design its heavy equipment from its own original designs rather than purchase an existing line. Three sizes were offered at first—the Models 110, 210, and 310 with 10, 18, and 27 heaped capacities, respectively. These three basic model designations were retained in the Michigan scraper line, and many variations and upgraded models appeared throughout the 1960s and 1970s.

In early 1964, Clark-Michigan aimed high by introducing the largest scraper ever to leave its shops, the Model 410. It was designed to compete with the Caterpillar 651, which had appeared a couple of years earlier. The massive 410 was slightly heavier than its competition, and it carried 44 cubic yards when heaped. The single-engine scraper was powered with a Cummins VT-1710-C diesel capable of producing 635 horsepower.

Unfortunately, sales of this machine proved disappointing, with only 20 units digging the dirt between 1964 and 1970, when it was discontinued.

In 1962, Allis-Chalmers began to expand its motor scraper line in a big way. Caterpillar had just launched its big 600-series, and Allis-Chalmers responded with the biggest scrapers it ever made, the Models TS-460 and 562 with 24 and 30 cubic yards struck capacity, respectively. The TS-460 topped out the Allis-Chalmers single-engine motor scraper line. The 562 was a twin-engine giant that could be operated with both engines for maximum horsepower capability or without the rear engine when assisted by a push-tractor. The 562 was discontinued in 1966, but the TS-460 evolved into the C model in 1968. It remained in production until Fiat of Italy purchased the majority of Allis-Chalmers in 1974 and the new Fiat-Allis joint venture was born.

At the top of the Michigan line of scrapers was this Model 410, which was launched in 1964. Carrying a heaped 44 cubic yards, it was powered by a single Cummins engine of 570 flywheel horsepower. *Volvo Construction Equipment*

Chapter 4

GRADERS

Graders are one of the earliest forms of earthmoving equipment. The earliest forms consisted of a simple board pulled by a horse. Animal power eventually gave way to mechanical power as steam tractors came into use at the end of the 19th century. Applying mechanical power to these flimsy graders was risky business. Designed to be horse-drawn, they simply disintegrated when pitted against the super power of the giant traction engines of the day. So manufacturers reacted by making pull-type graders heavier and better suited to the more powerful machines. When crawler tractors were invented in the early 1900s, they soon became a favorite to pull graders. In fact, pull-type graders survived well into the diesel tractor era and continued to find favor throughout the 1940s, but by the mid-1950s their production stopped. They were replaced by the more efficient motor graders, unrestricted by the slow speed of the crawler tractor and requiring one operator instead of two. Graders used to be called "patrols" or "maintainers" because their primary function was to patrol and maintain gravel roads.

Russell Grader Manufacturing Company brought out the first self-propelled, or motor, grader in 1919. Although primitive, it set the stage for Russell and other manufacturers to improve on the self-propelled idea, and soon all grader makers included self-propelled models in their lines. Caterpillar added graders to its product line when it purchased Russell in 1928.

Blade control on the early machines was by hand—usually through cranks, racks, and pinions operated by wheels at the operator's station. Hand control was tiresome and could be dangerous when the blade hit a solid object, so beginning in the 1920s graders began to appear with power controls. Most were mechanically controlled, though some manufacturers including Galion and Huber pioneered hydraulic controls at that time. But it took several decades before all grader manufacturers converted from mechanical to hydraulic controls.

Earthmoving equipment took to rubber tires in the late 1930s and hauling speeds of motor scrapers and off-highway trucks increased dramatically. As a result, graders became an essential tool to work with the earthmoving fleets.

The Komatsu GD825A is the flagship of the company's grader line. Its 16-foot blade, 280-horsepower engine, and 58,250-pound operating weight place it firmly in the heavyweight class. The first GD825A made its appearance at the 1987 Conexpo equipment show in Las Vegas, Nevada. *Komatsu Mining Systems*

The largest grader ever built was the colossal ACCO made by contractor Umberto Acco in Italy around 1980. This machine far exceeded in power and size anything resembling a grader before or since. It takes a 1,000-horsepower engine in the rear and a 700-horsepower engine up front to push the 33-foot blade. *Yvon LeCadre*

They were used not only for finishing slopes and spreading material for compaction, but also for maintaining dirt haul roads. A haulage fleet can only be used to its maximum potential when the haul road is smooth.

Graders are also an essential piece of equipment in surface mining operations, and it is here where the largest are found. Beginning in the 1960s, some colossal single-purpose graders were built to reclaim spoil piles and maintain roads for the largest off-highway trucks. Because these large graders sell in comparatively small numbers, manufacturers have tended to discontinue their production after a relatively short time. But Caterpillar, with its 16-series graders and introduction of the 24-H model in 1996, has persisted with its large graders and now dominates this market.

When the Galion Iron Works and Manufacturing Company announced the T-700 back in 1955, the company set a world size record for graders. Larger than anything else in

the grader industry, it boasted 190 horsepower and an operating weight of more than 40,000 pounds. The T-700 also boasted a power-shift transmission and a torque converter drive. Galion became a division of Dresser Industries Inc. in 1974. Then in 1988, the Komatsu Dresser Company joint venture was established. Komatsu's current largest grader is the GD825A-2 introduced in 1987. It weighs 58,250 pounds and carries a 280-horsepower engine.

In 1963, Caterpillar introduced the first of its big graders, the No.16 with 225 horsepower and a 14-foot blade. At 46,500 pounds, it became the largest grader on the market at that time. The No. 16 satisfied Caterpillar's large grader buyers for 10 years before it was followed by the 16G in 1973. With an articulated frame, 16-foot blade, power increased to 275 horsepower, and a weight of 60,150 pounds, this grader was even more popular than it predecessor. So popular, in fact, that the 16G remained in production for more than 20 years. In 1995 an updated 16H with a

Targeted for large surface mine haul roads, Caterpillar's massive 24-H was unveiled at the 1996 Minexpo mining show in Las Vegas, Nevada. At 131,000 pounds, and with an engine developing 500 horsepower, it was more than twice the weight of the existing largest grader on the market, Caterpillar's own 16-H. *Keith Haddock*

new operator's cab and electronically controlled transmission was launched.

The largest grader on the market at the turn of the millenium is the 24-H mining grader, which joined Caterpillar's lineup in 1996. This giant, weighing in at 131,000 pounds, ranks as one of the largest graders ever built and boasts a Caterpillar engine rated at 500 horsepower. Prior to the 24-H launch, Caterpillar's 16-H was the largest grader on the market. Thus, Caterpillar broke its own size record for graders and remains dominant in the big-grader market today.

In 1975, Dominion Road Machinery Company (Champion Road Machinery Ltd. from 1977) took a bold step with the introduc-

tion of the world's largest production-model grader, the 80-T. The Champion 80-T (which later became the 100-T) had an operating weight of 202,000 pounds and carried a 24-foot blade. Designed for use in surface mines to maintain roads for large haulers, or to reclaim vast areas of land, this machine was equipped with a 700-horsepower Cummins engine. This machine was offered for some 14 years, but few were sold.

The most familiar grader manufacturers did not make some of the largest graders. CMI Corporation, famous for its automated profiling and paving equipment, came out with a giant grader in 1969. Named the Autoblade, the 40-foot-long, double-articulated unit had

This outsize giant was the world's largest grader when unveiled in 1975. The Champion 100-T was powered by a 700-horsepower Cummins engine and weighed a massive 202,000 pounds. *Keith Haddock*

a power module at both ends, each consisting of a 225-horsepower diesel engine driving four wheels through hydrostatic drive. The eight-wheel-drive machine featured a centrally mounted cab that could rotate 180 degrees in either direction. In addition to heavy-duty grading, CMI also promoted the Autoblade as a precision grader, suitable for fine grad-

CMI Corporation produced this super grader, the Autoblade, in 1969. The 225-horsepower power modules at each end articulate on the main frame, and the cab module can swing 180 degrees—so either end can be the front. The machine illustrated is performing precise grade work as it automatically follows a preset grade line. *CMI Corporation*

ing in paving operations. The 65,000-pound machine could be guided in both alignment and grade from a fixed string line attached to pins on the ground.

RayGo Inc., famous for compactors, ventured into the super grader market in 1969 with a grader known as the Giant. It certainly lived up to its name. Like the CMI Autoblade, it was double-articulated and had a power unit at both ends, but at 106,000 pounds, the RayGo was some 60 percent heavier than the Autoblade. The power units at both ends were GM 318-horsepower diesel engines, each driving a single axle. Although the RayGo Giant was suitable for heavy-duty leveling and reclamation of surface mines, its blade was fixed to the central frame instead of the usual circle mounting. The operator's cab was mounted on the rear frame and suspended over the rear articulated joint, giving the operator a panoramic view of the blade and the front power unit. After the Giant had been tested and developed for several years by Ken Harris, a South Dakota contractor, RayGo began manufacturing in 1969. Raygo went out of business in 1985 when CMI Corporation purchased the company.

The RayGo "Giant" was one of the largest graders ever built. Weighing 53 tons, it featured double articulation and a 318-horsepower power unit at each end. This photo shows its front section turned 90 degrees and its blade fixed to the frame. *Keith Haddock*

O&K made its giant G350 motor grader from 1980 until 1986. This 90,000-pound machine had all the blade movements of the smaller grader but was designed to work with the largest haulers in surface mines. *Dave Wootton*

In 1980 Orenstein and Koppel (O&K) added a huge mining grader to its line of motor graders built in Germany for worldwide distribution. Known as the G-350, it weighed more than 90,000 pounds and was the largest grader at the time it was built. O&K sold 34 of the G-350 graders to many different countries, but in 1986 it dropped the model.

In 1980, Italian contractor Umberto ACCO created the world's largest grader ever. The one-of-a-kind 200-ton colossus was built for use on a major contract in Libya. With its 33-foot blade, front and rear engines totaling 1,700 horsepower, and 12 large tires, this colossal piece of equipment has dwarfed every other grader built to date.

Chapter 5

OFF-HIGHWAY TRUCKS

Pickup trucks, racing trucks, highway trucks, monster trucks—the English language has no words to truly describe the monster trucks of the earthmoving world. The word *truck* alone does not describe the off-highway variety. This kind of truck is so large that it can't legally travel on public roads and has to be broken down into pieces to be transported from job to job! These are the largest trucks ever to rumble across the earth.

Although the term *off-highway* implies that these trucks might be at home on rough, uneven roads, the opposite is in fact true: smooth and stable roads are essential to run these large vehicles efficiently. Frames can twist and crack running over uneven ground, so most open pit mines spend a great deal of effort on road maintenance to ensure their trucks run at the lowest cost per mile.

Before off-highway trucks were created, hauling vehicles were the highway type, built with light-duty frames, flimsy bodies (often

made of wood), and narrow wheels, which easily got stuck. By the early 1930s, the excavators that loaded these primitive trucks were comparatively better developed. As a result, the trucks were incompatible and ill-suited to handle the enormous loads of dirt and rock dropped from a shovel dipper, and then haul those full loads along unmade roads.

Some earlier attempts had been made to beef up highway truck designs, but it was the construction of the legendary Boulder Dam (now called the Hoover Dam) that bred true off-highway truck development in the early 1930s. Famous truck builder Mack redesigned some of its trucks for Boulder Dam use and then expanded into special off-road designs, which Mack continued to produce until 1981.

The off-highway truck filled a much-needed role in the earthmoving contractor's spread of equipment, and its success prompted many manufacturers to enter the field. Some were established truck makers, such as Dart and Mack, while others were specialist off-road vehicle builders. Experience proved that a highway-type truck could not be beefed up enough for regular off-highway service. It wasn't enough just to strengthen the frame and axles. Every component, including wheel rims, springs, door hinges, down to the last nut and bolt had to be designed to withstand

The largest trucks manufactured today carry 360 tons of material. Liebherr launched its contender, the T-282 electric-drive truck in 1998. It is three stories high to the canopy and more than 28 feet wide. A 2,700-horsepower MTU engine powers this behemoth. *Liebherr Mining Equipment Company*

The 260-ton-capacity Lectrahaul from Terex Mining was launched in 1995. It is powered by a 2,467-horsepower MTU diesel. This electric-drive truck is a descendant of a long line of electric trucks originally pioneered by the former Unit Rig and Equipment Company. *Eric C. Orlemann*

the most rugged usage on earthmoving and mining projects.

After World War II, truck sizes continued to increase to keep pace with the larger shovels loading them. The available size of engines, transmissions, and tires limited the development of larger trucks. This situation prompted Euclid to adopt twin power in the late 1940s, doubling up on engines, drivetrains, and drive axles to allow heavier loads to be carried.

In the 1960s, as stronger, more powerful components became available, truck design reverted to single-drive axle and single-engine designs. Tandem-drive trucks reappeared in the largest sizes in the early 1970s because the demand for increased capacity had once again overtaken technology available to produce large enough components. Today, tires and engines have now advanced to the point where the very largest trucks in production are once again single-drive axle and single-engine.

A major breakthrough came with the perfection of electric wheel drive, consisting of a diesel engine driving a generator, providing DC electric current to a motor in each driving wheel. R. G. LeTourneau developed one of the first electric haulers in conjunction with Anaconda Company of Butte, Montana. This was the trolley-assisted TR-60, a 75-ton articulated hauler, which left the LeTourneau plant in 1959. That same year, Unit Rig and Equipment Company brought out its prototype diesel-electric "Lectrahaul." The Lectrahaul line enjoyed immediate success and paved the way for general acceptance of the electric wheel drive truck in the world's surface mines. By 1979, the 2,500th Lectrahaul had been built and delivered, including fleets of the M-200, the world's largest truck when it came out in 1968. As a division of Terex Corporation from 1988, Unit Rig broke its own record again with the 260-ton MT-4400, the largest truck available when launched in 1995. Today, Unit Rig offers a range of trucks running up to its latest and largest, the MT-5500.

The 50-ton-capacity Euclid 1LLD was the world's largest truck in production in 1951. The version shown here was specially adapted to carry 150 tons by owner Western Contracting Corporation. It is receiving a load from another world record-beater, one of the firm's 10-yard Marion 191-M shovels. *Eric C. Orlemann collection*

It is equipped with AC electric wheel drive and is capable of carrying 340 tons.

The Dart Truck Company has built some massive off-highway trucks since its first in 1937. As early as 1951, Dart had already built a tandem-drive, 75-ton truck, a world-record beater for size. Then, in 1960, Dart came out with a 95-ton capacity, rear-dumping tractor-trailer unit known as the 95EDT. The Dart D2271, built in 1966, was the first mechanical drive truck with a regular two-axle configuration to break the 100-ton barrier. Dart was acquired in 1984 by Unit Rig and Equipment Company of Tulsa, Oklahoma.

Euclid Road Machinery Company of Euclid, Ohio, was the first company to specialize in haulers designed and built for off-highway duty, beginning in 1934. Following its twin-drive concept pioneered in the late 1940s, Euclid brought out the LLD 50-ton rear dump in 1951. Billed as the largest production truck in the world, the LLD was powered by two

This 1999 shot shows the largest Euclid truck ever built. The prototype R-280 is operating at Lehigh Coal's anthracite mine in Pennsylvania. The 280-ton unit is a diesel-electric hauler with A.C. motors in its rear wheels. Power comes from a single Detroit diesel that produces 2,500 horsepower. *Keith Haddock*

The famous Terex Titan (Model 33-19), at 350-tons capacity, held the title of the world's biggest truck for 25 years until 1999, when its capacity was exceeded by units from Caterpillar and Liebherr. The only 33-19 built has now finished its working days and stands preserved in the town of Sparwood, British Columbia, Canada, just a short distance from where it spent most of its working life. *Keith Haddock*

Cummins NHRS engines for a total of 600 horsepower. This successful truck became popular in open pit mines and earthmoving projects.

Other Euclid milestones include the 100-ton-class R-X in 1965, a rear dump hauler with a unique four-wheel-drive, articulated frame concept, and an experimental 210-ton-capacity truck in 1971, known as the R-210. This electric-powered vehicle was equipped with a gas turbine engine developing 1,850 horsepower.

After becoming a division of General Motors in 1953, Euclid has changed hands several times. Since 1992, the company has operated as Euclid-Hitachi Heavy Equipment Inc. Its current line of haulers is topped by the R-280, a diesel-electric truck powered by a Detroit S-4000 engine of 2,500 horsepower, and AC electric wheel drive.

The Terex name was born in 1968 because General Motors had to discontinue the manufacture and sale of off-highway trucks in the United States for a period of four years and give up the Euclid name following a Justice Department ruling. As a result, the name Terex was given to the continuing GM products, including trucks being made in the GM plant in Scotland and GM's other earthmoving equipment lines.

In 1972, GM re-entered the off-highway truck market with a new line of models

Big brother, little brother! The 35-ton-capacity Wabco Haulpak truck is shown against the colossal Haulpak 3200B, a 250-ton tandem-drive truck carrying a 2,000-horsepower General Motors locomotive engine. *Komatsu Mining Systems*

known as the 33-series. It included the colossal diesel-electric tandem-drive 33-19, known as the Titan, unveiled at the American Mining Congress Exhibition in Las Vegas in October 1974. At 350-ton capacity, it was the world's largest truck, a title it held for some 25 years. This behemoth measured almost 67 feet long by 26 feet wide, weighed 509,500 pounds empty, and boasted a GVW of 1,209,500 pounds. Using railroad diesel-electric drive technology, the Titan was powered by a 16-cylinder GM engine rated at 3,300 horsepower. The Titan ran on 10 tires measuring more than 11 feet in diameter. A unique feature was its rear bogie, which steered automatically with the front wheels to reduce tire scuffing. Today the Titan sits on display as a tourist attraction at Sparwood, British

A passenger vehicle follows this 320-ton Komatsu Haulpak 930E down a haul road at ASARCO's Ray Mine in Arizona. The top-of-the-line Komatsu hauler uses AC-drive wheel motors, which receive power from a motor-generator set developing 2,500 flywheel horsepower. *Keith Haddock*

Columbia, Canada, a short distance from the mine where it spent most of its working life. Just go to Sparwood—you can't miss it!

Terex today builds a line of articulated and rigid-frame off-highway trucks in its Scottish plant. The largest is the TR-100 of 100-ton capacity.

Today's Komatsu mining trucks derive their heritage from the LeTourneau-Westinghouse (Wabco) "Haulpak" truck line introduced in 1957. Their innovative offset cab and V-shaped body design became a standard feature for most off-highway trucks. The giant Wabco 3200 tandem-drive diesel-electric truck, equipped with a GM 645-E4 locomotive engine developing 2,000 horsepower, was launched in 1971. The truck measured 24 feet wide, 52 feet long, and could carry 250 tons.

In 1984, Wabco became a division of Dresser Industries Inc. Then in 1988, the Komatsu Dresser Company (KDC) joint venture was established. Since then Japan's Komatsu has acquired 100 percent interest in KDC. Today the trucks are marketed under Komatsu Mining Systems, and the "Haulpak" trade name still continues. The latest top-of-the-line truck from Komatsu Mining Systems is the 930E, with a payload rating up to 320 tons and maximum GVW of 1,059,000 pounds. Apart from its size, the real breakthrough on this vehicle is its electric wheel drive using AC motors. In fact, it was the first in the industry to do so. Launched at Minexpo Las Vegas in 1996, the 930E truck is 26 feet, 7 inches wide, 24 feet high, and more than 50 feet long.

This CH-300 is the largest of the Kress haulers built by the Brimfield, Illinois, company. Two of these 300-ton units are hauling coal at the Coteau Properties coal mine in North Dakota. As with all Kress haulers, the CH-300 features a rear-mounted engine, mechanical drive, and four straddle-mounted front wheels capable of turning 90 degrees to the frame. *Eric C. Orlemann*

The Kress Corporation of Brimfield, Illinois, makes the famous rigid-framed, bottom-dump coal carrier in size capacities from 110 to 300 tons, including the largest coal hauler of any type currently offered. Ted Kress founded the company in 1965, and in 1969 Ted's father, Ralph, joined him. Ralph played a major role in off-road truck development for more than three decades and had worked for Dart, Wabco, and Caterpillar. The first Kress haulers went to work in 1971 at the Captain Mine in Illinois. They were 150-ton, unitized (rigid-frame), bottom-dump haulers with rear engines and 180-degree steering. The CH-300 is the largest Kress truck sold to date and the largest single-unit coal hauler operating in 1999. Two CH-300 units are used at the Coteau Properties coal mine in North Dakota.

Kress' unique coal haulers are mechanically driven and designed to haul their large loads at high speeds—up to 60 miles per hour when the

Two trailers are better than one? Only in some conditions! Here two trailers combine to haul 270 tons at Peabody Coal Company's Lynville Mine in Indiana. The Rimpull Corporation of Olathe, Kansas, builds the unit. *Eric C. Orlemann collection*

road is smooth. The four front wheels, straddle-mounted in pairs, are capable of turning 90 degrees to the truck frame, allowing extremely tight turns in a narrow coal cut.

Rimpull is a company specializing in haulers for surface mining. Established in 1971, it produced a line of mechanical-drive haul trucks. "Back to Basics" was the company's slogan at a time when most manufacturers were promoting electric trucks with elaborate drive and suspension systems. By 1979 Rimpull offered a line consisting of five rear-dump models ranging from 65 to 120 tons in capacity and five tractor-trailer bottom-dump haulers ranging from 100 to 170 tons in capacity. Since then the line has expanded upward to include the 180-ton CW-180 and the CW-280, which presently hauls 300 tons of coal in a western mine. It is powered by

1,600-horsepower Detroit or Cummins engines.

Liebherr mining trucks appeared on the market in 1995 when Liebherr-America Inc. acquired Wiseda, a small company in Cardin, Oklahoma, that had built giant diesel-electric haul trucks since 1982. In 1985, the 2,000-horsepower Wiseda KL-2450 was the first truck in the industry to carry 240 tons on two axles. In the mid-1980s, Wisedas were sold to large mining operations in the United States and Australia.

Under Liebherr, the trucks have been redesigned, larger truck sizes added, and the models renumbered. The current T-series ranges in capacity from 200 to 360 tons. The top-of-the-line T-282, launched in 1998, features an AC wheel motor drive system, and a choice of MTU or Cummins engines that generate up to 3,200 horsepower. It is one of the largest trucks available today.

This 300-ton Liebherr TI-272 truck is an unusual design. The rear wheels are straddle-mounted in pairs, and there is no lateral support in the rear frame. The lower structural weight results in more payload carried per pound of truck. *Liebherr Mining Equipment Company*

The latest truck from Liebherr is the TI-272, a radical new design in the 300-ton class. It was designed from a clean slate with the objective of decreasing structural weight and thereby increasing payload-to-weight ratio. The design features four in-line rear wheels, straddle-mounted in pairs, and a rear frame with no lateral support. Necessary strength is provided by a beefed-up truck box.

Although Caterpillar's DW-series wheel tractors were pulling semi-trailer wagons as far back as 1941, the company didn't enter the off-highway truck business until 1962 with its Model 769. The 35-ton hauler featured stylish curves around the cab area, giving it a 1990s appearance. Later more models were introduced, including the hugely successful 85-ton 777 in 1975.

Caterpillar boosted the top end of its truck line with larger models during the 1980s, reaching a 240-ton capacity in 1990 with the Model 793. In 1998, Caterpillar announced its 797, a truck that would compete in the new 360-ton class, a world record, and capture the title held by the 350-ton Terex Titan since 1974. With the first fleets in operation by 1999, the 797 is 30 feet wide and boasts a gross vehicle weight of more than 1.2 million pounds. As with all Caterpillar's trucks, the 797 is equipped with mechanical drive and automatic power-shift transmission.

The real monster truck! This is Caterpillar's 797, a 360-ton mechanical-drive truck announced in 1998. It competes in the largest-size class offered today. It is 30 feet wide, has a 3,400-horsepower Caterpillar engine, and has a GVW of 1,230,000 pounds. *Caterpillar Inc.*

Chapter 6

LARGE CABLE EXCAVATORS

The cable-operated excavator was one of the earliest machines ever to move earth. The 1835 steam shovel, designed by William S. Otis, is the first documented excavator used on land. It was rail-mounted and carried a 1-cubic-yard dipper mounted on a boom and arm that swung through a half circle. The primary use for these machines in the 19th century was railroad construction, so they became known as "railroad shovels," but up to the latter part of the 19th century, only a few steam shovels were built. Most of the work was still done by hand labor. The idea of mechanized excavation caught on slowly because of closely protected patents held by the Otis family and because labor was cheap and plentiful.

These first machines used chains to operate the shovel movements; later machines used steel cables. This type of machine soon became known as the cable excavator. Today this name still distinguishes them from the modern hydraulic excavator.

In the 1920s, gasoline- and oil-powered machines became popular. Until then, steam had been the primary power for most excavators. Also in the 1920s, the full-swing or fully revolving heavy-duty mining shovel finally replaced the railroad shovel. Examples of fully revolving shovels had appeared at the end of the 19th century, but they were usually small and not tough enough to work in quarries and mines.

The introduction of the first fully revolving quarry and mine shovel by Bucyrus in 1925 revolutionized the heavy excavation industry. The 4-yard Bucyrus 120-B, an electric-powered shovel, was designed to tackle the heaviest excavation. Designed to load trucks or rail wagons, the 120-B was the real forerunner of today's mining shovels.

Today, medium and small cable excavators have been all but replaced by hydraulic excavators (chapter 10), but in the larger sizes, cable shovels still hold their own. The boom in surface mining in the 1970s brought larger two-crawler shovels to load the larger trucks then available. This trend

---

The first quarry and mine shovel was the Bucyrus-Erie 120-B. It was introduced in 1925 as a 5-yard electric shovel. For the first time, a fully revolving shovel embodied the ruggedness of the part-swing railroad shovel, and a new class of machine was created. *Komatsu Mining Systems*

It all started with the steam shovel, the forerunner of all modern cable-operated shovels. A 3/4-yard Erie B is demonstrated at a Historical Construction Equipment Association open day at Bowling Green, Ohio. *Keith Haddock*

has continued in the 1990s, and even larger trucks, well over 300 tons, were developed. Since customers demand 3- to 4-pass loading of these huge trucks, shovel manufacturers have responded with ever-larger two-crawler electric shovels.

Lima Locomotive Works of Lima, Ohio, established a well-favored line of crawler excavators since its origins in the Ohio Power Shovel Company in 1928. In 1943 it built two Model 1600s, which were large crawler cranes. In 1948, the 1600 graduated to the Model 2400, a diesel-powered machine of heavy proportions. It featured air-controlled clutches and brakes and was initially offered as a

6-yard shovel or dragline. The 2400 became the mainstay of Lima's range of excavators and crawler cranes. With its distinctive appearance, clean lines, and curved-house design, the 2400 is a favorite among many shovel enthusiasts. A reliable machine in the field, it used to be popular with coal stripping contractors in the eastern United States and in the United Kingdom.

After several name changes, the Lima company was purchased by Clark Equipment Company in 1971, and its excavators became known as Clark-Lima. In 1969, the 2400 was upgraded to an 8-yard capacity and designated as the 2400B. Because of dwindling sales of this size of cable excavator, manufacturing was discontinued in 1981.

As one of the pioneering steam shovel manufacturers, Marion Power Shovel Company was established in 1884 as the Marion Steam Shovel Company at Marion, Ohio. Marion grew into one of the foremost manufacturers of excavating machines, competing with its arch rival, Bucyrus, in making products such as railroad shovels, dredges, cranes, walking draglines, and drills.

In the 1960s, Marion gradually pulled away from the small-machine market, preferring to concentrate on large two-crawler excavators bigger than the 10-yard-class, walking draglines, and blast hole drills.

With the sale of the first 191-M in 1951, Marion took the title for the world's largest shovel on two crawlers. (See top picture on page 45.) This 10-yard shovel was diesel-powered, with three engines totaling 1,700 horsepower. Other 191-Ms were electric-powered. The 191-M was a successful machine for Marion, and repeat orders were received from mines and contractors around the world up to 1989, by which time its standard dipper had grown to 15 cubic yards.

In an effort to increase the dipper capacity of its shovels, Marion designed the unusual "Superfront" shovel with a claimed increase of 66 percent over its standard dipper size. After a seven-year testing program, the Superfront

The Lima 2400 was one of the largest diesel-powered cable shovels. It carried an 8-yard dipper and was popular with small and medium mine operators. The one shown here is removing overburden at a British surface coal mine in 1988. *Dave Wootton*

The Marion 301-M was designed to load 240-ton trucks in three passes with its 57-cubic-yard dipper. First appearing in 1985, it was upgraded to the 351-M in 1995. Following Marion's takeover by Bucyrus, this machine is still available as the Bucyrus 595-B. *Eric C. Orlemann*

was announced in 1974. The Superfront's increased capacity comes from its geometry and the weight saved by replacing the boom with a stiff leg. Its digging action causes the hoist and crowd motions to work together as the dipper moves up the bank, exerting large crowd forces. The production model Superfront was known as the 204-M and was offered with a standard 30-cubic-yard dipper.

To keep pace with the increasing size of off-highway trucks, Marion designed the 301-M, a 57-yard shovel designed to load 240-ton

trucks in three passes. The first of these 1,150-ton shovels was sold in 1985. In 1995, the 301-M was upgraded to the 351-M, and it became Marion's largest two-crawler shovel. With dipper range similar to its predecessor, its weight was upped to 1,300 tons.

In 1997, the Marion Power Shovel Company was purchased by Bucyrus International Inc. (formerly Bucyrus-Erie Company). The merger of these two giants was a significant event in the earthmoving industry and ended 113 years of competition, sometimes fiercely

For three-pass loading of 170-ton trucks, Harnischfeger's P&H 4100A electric mining shovel has been the top seller since its introduction in 1991. The 56-yard shovel, shown here at ASARCO's Mission Mine, Arizona, is one of many in the copper mines in the western United States. *Keith Haddock*

This Bucyrus 395-B shovel is removing overburden from tar sands at the Syncrude mining operation near Fort McMurray, Alberta, Canada. Note the super-wide tracks on this particular machine to minimize sinking in the soft material. The 395-B was introduced in 1979 as a 34-yard electric shovel. *Keith Haddock*

fought, between the two rivals. The creation of the new company reduced the number of manufacturers supplying the Western world with electric cable-operated shovels and walking draglines (chapter 8) from three to just two—Bucyrus and P&H.

Since its establishment in 1880 as the Bucyrus Foundry and Manufacturing Company, the present-day Bucyrus International Inc. of South Milwaukee, Wisconsin, can boast a rich heritage of specialization in the crane and excavator industry. From the smallest yard crane to some of the largest machines ever to roam the earth, no other company has built such a wide variety of types and sizes of excavating machines as those built over the past century by Bucyrus.

Bucyrus-Erie's large two-crawler loading shovels were a natural progression from its smaller excavators and filled the gap between these and its giant stripping shovels. In the early 1950s, the entire Bucyrus line of electric shovels was replaced by the 110-B, 150-B, and 190-B models, ranging in size up to 9 cubic yards. From here the trend was upward in size, to keep pace with the largest trucks as they became available.

The 21-yard 295-B was introduced in 1972 and was popular for more than a decade. The 34-yard 395-B, the first to use AC motors and B-E's patent computerized "Acutrol" control, followed in 1979. The present two-crawler shovel range spans from the 195-B to the 595-B. This latter machine, with a dipper capacity range from 40 to 80 cubic yards, was inherited from Marion and was previously known as the 351-M. Bucyrus has kept it in production since the Marion takeover.

The other player in the large electric excavator stakes is Harnischfeger Corporation (P&H), coincidentally from Milwaukee, Bucyrus' hometown. The present line of P&H large crawler shovels and draglines has a long pedigree dating back to the company's founding by Alonzo Pawling and Henry Harnischfeger in 1884. The company built its first excavator, the gasoline-powered 1 1/4-yard Model 210, in 1914. Its first electric shovel, the 1200WL, appeared in 1933. With a 2-yard capacity, it was the forerunner of today's P&H mining shovel line. The company persisted in the electric mining shovel market, gaining the necessary expertise to boost it into a dominant position in terms of mining shovel sales. Their popular 15-yard 2100 series electric shovels introduced in 1961, the 25- to 30-yard 2800 introduced in 1969, and the 56-yard 4100 introduced in 1991 have all been big sellers for P&H. At the time of this writing, the P&H 5700XPA in the 70-yard class ranks as the world's largest excavator on two crawlers.

Holding the distinction of the world's largest excavator on two crawlers, the P&H 5700XPA weighs in at 2,100 tons and carries a nominal dipper of 80 cubic yards. R. W. Miller and Company took delivery of this one in 1991 for work in New South Wales, Australia. *P&H Mining Equipment*

Chapter 7

STRIPPING SHOVELS

Stripping shovels are the true giants of the mobile machine world. These huge machines include the 15,000-ton "Captain" shovel, the heaviest piece of equipment ever to move under its own power on land. Only the largest ships on the ocean have a greater movable mass than these monster machines.

The largest stripping shovels are found in surface coal mines; smaller sizes were also located in limestone and ironstone quarries. Stripping shovels work the same way as the cable shovels described in chapter 6, but they have longer booms and don't deposit their load onto another vehicle. Regular shovels load haulage trucks, which carry the material away. However, the gigantic proportions of the stripping shovel with its longer boom allow it to dig from a high face, swing around, and pile the material clear of the working area. In surface coal mines these machines dig long strips or cuts and cast the material into the adjacent cut from which the coal has

already been removed. It's similar to large-scale plowing of a field where the furrow being cut is turned over into the adjacent furrow. After the shovel has passed through, bulldozers level the piles of spoil, scrapers replace the subsoil and topsoil, and the land is then put back to productive use.

Large stripping shovels are mounted on eight crawler tracks arranged in pairs, one pair at each corner of the lower frame. Each two-crawler assembly is attached to a large vertical hydraulic cylinder for leveling the machine, an important feature when negotiating uneven ground. The leveling is usually done automatically: A pendulum system directs the hydraulic fluid to and from the four cylinders to keep the machine on an even keel. The front and rear crawler assemblies are steered independently by horizontal hydraulic rams.

Operating a large stripping shovel is a precise science that takes careful planning. Because of the high ground pressure under its crawlers, the stripping shovel must always operate on a very stable footing, such as the coal it has uncovered. If the stripping shovel ran off the solid material it would soon become stuck. When the biggest machine on the site gets stuck, nothing can pull it out. It may take several days for other equipment to excavate

From the floor of a mine, the Marion 5860 is truly an impressive sight. This giant stripping shovel has a working weight of 10,150,000 pounds and features a 180-foot boom that carries an 80 cubic-yard bucket. The giant bucket's inside dimensions are 11 feet high; 12 feet, 6 inches deep; and 14 feet wide.

Stripping shovels reached 12-cubic-yards capacity by 1927. This example is the Bucyrus-Erie 750-B uncovering coal at the Utility Mine, Saskatchewan, Canada. It was one of the first to be mounted on crawler tracks. *Keith Haddock*

around the large shovel and haul in dry material until the huge machine can be driven out under its own power.

Of course, these large machines must be dismantled into "small" pieces when they are moved from one site to another. Some shovels have been dismantled and re-erected several times during their lives. A new machine may need more than 250 truck or rail car loads of parts to complete delivery.

The first long boom (stripping) shovel, as we know it today, was a fully revolving 78-ton machine built in 1900 by John H. Wilson and Company in England. It worked in iron-stone mining and carried a dipper of 1 1/2-cubic-yard capacity on a 70-foot-long boom. This first machine was so successful, it worked for 54 years! Other stripping shovels followed in England. Then the first in the United States appeared in 1911 when Marion built its Model 250. That was a steam-powered, rail-mounted machine weighing 150 tons and carrying a 3 1/2-yard dipper on a 65-foot boom.

The Bucyrus 320-B, released in 1925, was the first stripping shovel to be equipped with crawler tracks. Interestingly, the 320-B was introduced a year earlier as a 7 1/2-yard rail-mounted machine. The four rail trucks were replaced with eight crawler tracks mounted in pairs at each corner. Marion quickly responded by mounting one of their stripping shovels on crawler tracks later the same year. They chose their Model 350, an 8-yard shovel that held the world's record for size when introduced in 1923.

By 1930 most stripping shovels were ordered with crawler tracks, and rail mounting became obsolete due to its lack of mobility. Up until the mid-1920s, these mighty shovels were powered by steam or electricity. Since then, they have been exclusively electric-powered.

Advances in size continued, and both Marion and Bucyrus introduced stripping shovels of 12-cubic yards capacity in 1927. For Marion, it was the 5480, weighing just less than 1,000 tons and incorporating most of the features already proven on the 350. For Bucyrus, it was the 750-B, forerunner of a long line of giant stripping shovels produced by that company.

For the next four decades, Marion and Bucyrus vied with each other to produce the world's largest machine, the title passing from one to the other many times. Launched in 1935, the Bucyrus-Erie 950-B had a host of

Probably the most famous of the big stripping shovels was the Mountaineer (Marion 5760), shown here with Paul Bunyan in this artist's rendering. Going to work in 1955, it was the first of the super strippers built in the 1960s and 1970s. It broke all records with its 60-yard dipper and 2,750-ton operating weight. *Dimitrie Toth Jr. collection*

The 3850-B is the largest shovel ever built by Bucyrus-Erie. The photo shows one of the two purchased by Peabody Coal Company. It's the 140-cubic-yard machine at the River King Mine, Illinois, which started work in 1964. This colossal machine weighed 9,000 tons, and its boom towered 250 feet above ground—90 feet higher than the Statue of Liberty. *Bucyrus International Inc.*

innovations. Not only did its 30-yard dipper break the size record, it also had many features that have remained in Bucyrus shovel design ever since. Most notable was the front-end arrangement with a single tubular dipper handle operated by wire ropes and a two-part boom pinned at its center and tied to the gantry with two heavy beams. The tubular handle allowed the dipper to rotate and alleviate stresses on the handle and boom. A propel motor in each of the four crawler assemblies eliminated the previous complicated system of multiple gear trains, shafts, and chains.

Here are two of the largest pieces of iron ever to work in a single pit. The scene is at Arch Coal Company's Captain Mine, Illinois, where the Marion 6360 shovel in the foreground, the largest shovel ever built, stands 21 stories high. Its 15,000 tons are needed to maneuver its 180-cubic-yard dipper through rocky overburden. Beside the tracks notice the wheel loader used to remove stray boulders. In the background, the largest cross-pit bucket wheel excavator in North America assists with the softer, upper part of the overburden. *Eric C. Orlemann*

Another breakthrough was Marion's "Knee Action" crowd in 1940. On this shovel, the dipper handle was connected to a movable stiff leg instead of the boom. This helped to eliminate torsional and bending stresses from the boom so it could be made much lighter. The knee-action crowd was first fitted to the new Model 5561, which, at 35-cubic-yards capacity, claimed a dipper size record yet again. Nicknamed the "grasshopper" front because the long handle and stiff leg appeared to fold like the insect's leg, the Knee Action crowd became standard for all Marion stripping shovels and some later Bucyrus machines.

The era of the "super strippers" began in 1956 when the Mountaineer, the Marion 5760 monster shovel, took its first bite of earth in eastern Ohio. As high as a 16-story building, this behemoth could take a dipper load of 60 cubic yards from a face, then deposit it a football field away and stack it 10 stories high. It even had an elevator inside to carry the crew from ground to cab level. The 2,750-ton Mountaineer drew much worldwide publicity and was probably the most famous of the big strippers. Yet people attending its launching ceremony would never have suspected that in only a decade, a shovel exactly three times bigger would be built by the same manufacturer.

More massive strippers appeared in the 1950s, then came a huge jump in size. Bucyrus-Erie took the spotlight in 1960 by announcing its order for the world's largest shovel. This was the 3850-B with a dipper capacity of 115 cubic yards, almost double the size of the largest shovel then in operation. Within a year, a second 3850-B was under construction. This time the boom was some 10 feet shorter, but the dipper capacity was correspondingly increased to 140 cubic yards. The second 3850-B started work in 1964. Both 3850-Bs had operating weights between 9,000 and 10,000 tons and were the largest ever built by the Bucyrus-Erie Company.

Another super stripper was Bucyrus-Erie's 1850-B with a 90-yard dipper on a 150-foot boom. Named Big Brutus, the 5,500-ton shovel went to work near West Mineral, Kansas, in 1963. After only 11 years of work, this modern machine was idled but not scrapped. It now stands high and proud on public display near West Mineral, having been restored by Big Brutus Inc., a nonprofit organization dedicated to its preservation.

The race for the largest stripping shovel ended in 1965 when Marion broke the final record for shovel size. The incredible Marion 6360, named the Captain, truly was the captain of all shovels. This mammoth mining shovel is still the largest machine of any type to move under its own power on land. It stood 21 stories high, weighed more than 15,000 tons, and its bucket carried 180 cubic yards. Overall, the 6360 shovel looked like most other Marion stripping shovels, but what set this shovel apart were its gigantic proportions. It was propelled on four pairs of crawlers at a top speed of 1/4 mile per hour, using two electric motors in each pair. Its crawler assemblies were 16 feet high, with each crawler shoe measuring 10 feet across and tipping the scales at 3 1/2 tons.

The life of the Captain shovel ended abruptly on September 9, 1991, when a disastrous fire raged for several hours in its lower works. Damaged beyond repair, the colossal machine was scrapped in late 1992. During its lifetime, the 6360 shovel moved about 810 million cubic yards of overburden, more than three times the quantity of material excavated for the Panama Canal.

There were no more record-breakers after the Captain, but several other stripping shovels were built. Bucyrus-Erie commissioned two 1950-Bs in Ohio in 1965 and 1967 with 130- and 105-yard capacity dippers. The latter is the Silver Spade, one of

only a handful of stripping shovels still operating today. The very last stripping shovel, a 105-yard Marion 5900, started work in 1971.

Despite its immense size, the stripping shovel is limited to the depth of overburden it can remove. Unlike a dragline, which can work on the surface and move into advantageous positions to gain dumping reach, the shovel must sit on the coal in the bottom of the cut where its movement and range are limited. As "shallow" coal reserves are exhausted, stripping shovels have been retired at a rapid rate, and none have been built since 1971.

Except for a few stripping shovels built in the former Soviet Union and some smaller strippers built by Ransomes and Rapier in England, all the large stripping shovels were built by Marion or Bucyrus. The intense rivalry between these two companies goes back to their founding in the 1880s, so it was a major event in 1997 when Bucyrus International Inc. purchased the Marion Power Shovel Company. This merger ended a rivalry that had lasted 113 years.

The Silver Spade was the first of two Bucyrus-Erie 1950-Bs purchased by Consolidation Coal Company for work in southeastern Ohio. Its dipper holds 105 cubic yards, and the boom towers 200 feet above ground level. The 1950-B was the only Bucyrus-Erie shovel to be equipped with "knee-action" crowd, originally a Marion patent. *Keith Haddock*

73

Chapter 8

WALKING DRAGLINES

Walking draglines are large digging machines usually found in surface mines, sand and gravel pits, or limestone quarries. They belong to a family of excavators that includes some of the most massive machines ever to move on land. These monster machines can move vast quantities of earth to uncover coal and other valuable minerals. And they have to be reliable machines because they are usually called upon to work around the clock for almost every day of the year.

A walking dragline looks like a large crane, but instead of carrying a hook to lift loads, it carries a digging bucket suspended on the end of its boom by hoist ropes. In action, the bucket is dragged toward the machine by another set of ropes, called drag ropes, as it collects its load. When full, the bucket is hoisted, the machine swings, and the load is dumped in a pile to the side. To swing, the machine revolves on a large roller

bearing on a circular base on which the machine sits while digging. In surface mining operations, the material is usually dumped into the empty cut alongside where the mineral has already been extracted.

Since it began in the last century, the surface mining industry has needed excavators that move immense amounts of material efficiently, and the walking dragline does the job perfectly. Where the excavated material is to be deposited within the range of the machine, and where the geology of a site permits, a dragline usually is the most efficient machine for bulk excavation.

The first dragline machine was home-built by Page and Schnable, a contractor working on the Chicago Drainage Canal in 1904. Following its success, Page and others started building the new type of excavator. These early machines were mounted on rails or on skids and rollers and pulled themselves along by means of their bucket, a slow and clumsy method. Starting in 1911, some draglines became self-propelling when fitted with crawler tracks. Then, in 1913, Oscar Martinson of the Monighan Machine Company invented the radical idea of attaching two movable shoes, one on each side of the dragline's revolving frame. This innovation forever changed the way draglines move.

This is one of the P&H Model 9020 draglines shipped to Australia. It started work at Peabody's Bengalla Mine, New South Wales, in 1998. It is carrying a 75-yard bucket on a 390-foot boom. *P&H Mining Equipment*

The 22-yard Bucyrus-Erie 1150-B is stacking the overburden as high as it can at Saint Aidans coal mine near Leeds, England, in 1986. Originally built in 1948, the 1,220-ton dragline is now preserved at the site as a tourist attraction. At the time of writing, it is the only walking dragline in the world to be preserved. *Keith Haddock*

The walking system is simple. To take a step, an eccentric drive rotates the shoes in a circular motion, so they both touch the ground at the same time. Further rotation lifts the leading edge of the dragline's circular tub off the ground, pulls it ahead the distance of one step, and then lowers the machine gently back on its base. The shoes continue to rotate, and the process is repeated step by step. Walking draglines always walk backward, because they are designed to walk away from the cut being made. Changing direction (steering) is just a matter of pointing the rear of the machine in the desired direction when the shoes are off the ground.

This is the Marion 8900 purchased by Peabody Coal Company for work in Indiana in 1967. Now carrying a 155-cubic-yard bucket, the photo shows a scene at the Hawthorne Mine with a 95-yard Bucyrus-Erie 2570-W in the background. *Eric C. Orlemann*

Because of its size, a walking dragline must be dismantled into many "small" pieces to move to another job. Most mining operations last so long, however, that the high cost of dismantling and erecting these giant machines is insignificant when averaged over their lifetime of 30 years or more.

In 1932, dragline builder Monighan, with its patented propel system, was taken over by Bucyrus-Erie Company (now Bucyrus Inter-national Inc.). The company soon designed larger draglines incorporating Monighan patents. The Bucyrus-Erie 950-B, the world's largest in 1935, swung a 12-yard bucket on a 250-foot boom. This machine was developed into the 1150-B, a 25-yard machine of massive proportions, the first of which moved earth in 1945.

The British firm of Ransomes and Rapier Ltd. unveiled the W170, its first dragline, in

Dragline Bucket Dwarfs Caterpillar D9 Dozer! This is the 130-yard bucket hanging from the Marion 8900 dragline at the Moura Mine, Queensland, Australia, soon after it went to work in 1967. The mine was a Thiess-Peabody-Mitsui joint venture. *Biloela Studios*

The Marion Steam Shovel Company entered the walking dragline market in 1939 with the Model 7200, swinging a 5-yard bucket on a 120-foot boom. The 7200 and the 11-yard Model 7400 launched the following year paved the way for Marion to unveil the world's largest walking dragline in 1942. A huge machine for its day, the 7800 could carry 30 cubic yards on a 185-foot boom.

Bigger draglines followed in the 1960s, the decade of the big strippers. Marion startled the dragline world with the introduction of its Model 8800 in 1963. This world-record beater represented a massive jump in size, with its 6,000-ton operating weight and 85-yard bucket on a 275-foot boom. Two larger Marion 8900s followed, one sent to Australia in 1966 and the other to a coal mine in Indiana the next year. These carried 130- and 145-yard buckets. The Indiana 8900 was upgraded to a 155-yard bucket in 1993. Marion's largest dragline was the 150-yard 8950. Only one was built and went to work in southern Indiana in 1973.

Big Muskie (Model 4250-W), the most famous and biggest of all draglines, gained Bucyrus-Erie Company the crowning glory of the largest bucket ever to swing from an excavator. Launched in 1969, Big Muskie had a massive 220-cubic yard-capacity and 310-foot boom. With an estimated operating weight of 15,000 tons, it housed 32 D.C. generators, powering 10 hoist motors, 8 drag motors, and 10 swing motors, a total of 48,500 horsepower.

From its beginnings already mentioned, Page Engineering Company modernized its draglines in the mid-1950s and started to build its 700-series. The most popular was the Model 752, swinging a standard 42-yard bucket. Many of these dug in the Midwestern coal mines and the Florida phosphate fields. Page's largest dragline was the Model 757 delivered in 1983 to a coal mine in Alberta, Canada. Weighing 4,500 tons, it carries a 75-cubic-yard bucket.

1938. It carried a 4-yard bucket on a 135-foot boom. Larger machines followed, and by 1951 the Rapier W1400 at 1,880 tons operating weight and 282-foot boom, won the title of the world's largest dragline. The "world's largest" title was claimed again by Rapier in 1961 when it launched the W1800. This machine weighed 2,000 tons and carried a bucket of 40 cubic yards. Bucyrus International purchased the patents and manufacturing rights of Ransomes and Rapier walking draglines in 1988.

Marion's largest dragline, the one and only 8950, was purchased by Amax Coal Company and put to work at the Ayrshire Mine, Indiana. The colossal machine swung a bucket of 150 cubic yards on a 310-foot boom and weighed 7,300 tons. *Keith Haddock*

In 1988, Page Engineering Company was purchased by Harnischfeger Corporation (P&H), giving the latter a line of draglines to add to its popular shovels. The first P&H dragline was sold to a coal mine in England. Commissioned in 1991, it was an updated version of the Model 757. P&H has since redesigned its draglines and assembled the first of its new 9000-series machines in Australia. The Model 9020 swings a 115-yard bucket on a 320-foot boom. It went to work in 1996 in New South Wales, Australia.

Other new large walking draglines going to work in the 1990s include the 160-yard Bucyrus-Erie 2570-WS dragline with a 360-foot boom at the Black Thunder Mine in Wyoming, the Marion 8750 with its 106-yard bucket on the world's longest boom (420 feet) at Fording Coal's Genesee Mine in Alberta, Canada, and Luscar's P&H 9020 starting work at the end of the millennium at the Boundary

The Big Muskie (Bucyrus-Erie 4250-W) is the most famous of all the draglines. With a 220-cubic-yard capacity, it was the largest dragline ever built and one of the largest machines ever to move on land. Central Ohio Coal Company operated the machine in southern Ohio. Note the two men at the top of the boom. Unfortunately, the machine was cut up for scrap in 1999. *Keith Haddock*

Dragline booms don't come any longer than this one. The Marion 8750 at the Fording Coal Ltd. Genesee operations in Alberta, Canada, swings a 106-cubic-yard bucket on a boom measuring 420 feet long. Electric motors on this machine total almost 38,000 horsepower. *Fording Coal Ltd.*

Ursa Major (Bucyrus-Erie 2570-WS) operates a 160-yard bucket on a 360-foot boom at the Black Thunder Mine, Wyoming. It is the largest dragline operating in the world today and the fourth largest ever built. *Bucyrus International*

Dam Mine, Saskatchewan, Canada, carrying a 98-cubic-yard bucket.

As with the stripping shovels described in the last chapter, the large walking dragline industry was dominated by Bucyrus and Marion over many decades until 1997. The rivalry ended when Bucyrus International Inc. purchased the Marion Power Shovel Company. The Marion plant in Ohio closed, and the manufacturing rights to the Marion machines transferred to the Bucyrus plant at South Milwaukee, Wisconsin.

Fireworks and fanfare celebrate a new dragline! The Model 757 built by Harnischfeger Corporation (P&H) was launched in December 1991. It went to work at the British Coal Opencast Stobswood Mine in northern England, uncovering coal with its 65-yard bucket. *Peter Grimshaw collection*

Chapter 9

BUCKET WHEELS
AND OTHER CONTINUOUS EXCAVATORS

As the name implies, continuous excavators are digging machines that move material in one continuous stream—no stopping! This is in contrast to all other types of earthmoving machines that operate in cycles: excavators that dig, swing, then dump; bulldozers that must back up after each push; and haulers that must return empty after each load.

Continuous excavators come in many varieties, from the small ditching machines seen on subdivision housing projects to the giant bucket wheel excavators that are some of the largest self-propelled machines ever constructed. Several of these giants are working in Germany and can excavate more than 300,000 tons of material per day. That output exceeds the capability of any other single machine yet built.

The elevating grader was one of the earliest continuous digging machines. Initially pulled by teams of horses, later by tractors, the elevating grader consisted of a cutting blade or disk, which directed the material onto a driven belt suspended from the frame. The continuous stream of earth could be discharged into wagons running alongside, or formed into windrows for compaction into a road base.

By the mid-1940s, most grader manufacturers had discontinued the elevating types in favor of nimble motor scrapers and regular graders with greater capability. Nevertheless, the principle of the elevating grader—a machine moving along a cut continuously excavating and loading a stream of material—lives on in today's giant surface miners.

Surface miners are self-propelled machines that work in a similar manner to the elevating grader, but most types use a powerful cutting wheel capable of excavating hard material by its milling action. Surface miners are capable of extremely high output. In fact, when loading trucks, operators often have difficulty providing enough trucks to cope with the surface miner's insatiable appetite. Another advantage is their ability to peel off thin layers of material in mining operations or separate partings from the mineral.

The Euclid BV Loader unveiled at the 1948 Chicago Road Show was, in effect, the first surface miner, and thus attracted a lot of attention. Designed to be pulled by the largest

One of the largest bucket wheel excavators built by Krupp also works at Rheinbraun's Hambach Mine. It can dig to the height of a 16-story building. Note the operator's cab suspended below the boom near the wheel. *Krupp Fordertechnik*

This is the business end of a MAN/Takraf machine. The wheel alone measures 71 feet in wheel diameter and has 18 buckets of 8 cubic yards each. Note the position of the operator's cab on the boom. *Yvon LeCadre*

crawler tractors of the day, the BV loader was mounted on a pair of nonpowered crawler tracks. Its main frame supported a blade that simply cut the material and directed it onto its conveyor belt. The material was discharged off the belt and into haul trucks moving alongside.

In the mid-1970s, CMI Corporation of Oklahoma City, Oklahoma, developed some coal-loading surface miners from its line of pavement profilers. The machines featured a centrally mounted cutting drum with a powerful milling action, able to dig hard coal without ripping or blasting.

Another type of continuous excavator developed by CMI was the Autovator 1000. Two 425-horsepower diesel engines propelled eight hydrostatically driven crawler track assemblies on this spectacular machine. The 90-ton machine could dig up to 240 feet per minute and excavate up to 6,000 cubic yards per hour. That's enough to fill more than 300 regular-size tandem trucks. The Autovator sliced material from a face at one side of the machine and loaded it from a discharge conveyor at the other side.

Another machine that cuts a vertical slice of material is the Holland Loader. It consists of a 15-foot-high cutting blade and an 8-foot-wide main conveyor. The entire machine is suspended on a frame, supported between two large crawler tractors that provide the cutting and propelling power. The frame can be raised or lowered hydraulically. The sheer brute force of the tractors combined with the 525-horsepower of the engine driving the conveyor produce high outputs of excavation—up to 7,000 cubic yards per hour. Holland Loaders are usually coupled between two of the largest crawler tractors available: first Caterpillar D9Gs, then D9Hs

The Autovator, built by CMI Corporation, is shown taking a slice of earth and placing it in neat windrows. However, its main purpose is to load trucks on the go. It has two engines of 425 horsepower each, eight crawler tracks, and two cabs so the operator can choose the best view of the work. *CMI Corporation*

The spectacular Holland Loader has lots of horsepower. In addition to the two Fiat-Allis 41-B tractors of 520 horsepower each, one pulling and one pushing, there is a 525-horsepower engine driving the conveyor. It can load a 100-ton truck in less than a minute. *Holland Loader Company*

This Bucyrus-Erie, built on the base of an old Marion shovel, is one of the few bucket wheel excavators designed and built in North America. Known as the 5872-WX, it started work at the Captain Mine Arch Coal Company, Illinois, in 1986. Unfortunately, the mine closed in 1998, and the machine was scrapped the following year. *Eric C. Orlemann*

Another continuous excavator is the Krupp KSM 2000R. It features a cutting wheel at the front and diesel power of 1,340 horsepower. The one shown here is at the Taldinskij Mine in Russia. *Krupp Canada*

or Fiat-Allis HD-41s. Most recently, a pair of Caterpillar D11Ns are being used. In this configuration, the combined power of the two tractors, plus the conveyor engine, runs to a massive 2,065 horsepower.

The line of Surface Miners made by Krupp Fordertechnik GmbH of Germany, includes the largest yet produced. First available in 1988, these machines have a rotating wheel at the front of the machine, and material is discharged to the rear via a conveyor that can swing through an arc of 200 degrees. Mounted on a pair of crawler tracks, the entire upper frame pivots at the rear, so the digging wheel can be raised and lowered by two hydraulic cylinders at the front of the crawler frame.

The record-beating KSM 4000 machine was tested in 1991 and 1992 at a Wyoming coal mine. With 3,100 horsepower, the machine weighed 419 tons and was designed to excavate more than 5,000 cubic yards per hour. More recently, Krupp and the Russian Institute of Mining have jointly developed a prototype of the smaller KSM 2000. Of similar design to its larger brother, the KSM 2000 is outfitted with diesel power of 1,340 horsepower. The machine completed successful performance tests in June 1996 and was handed over to the Taldinskij Mine in Russia.

The bucket wheel excavators (BWEs), originating in Europe in the early 1900s, are the largest continuous excavators. Early bucket wheel machines borrowed their technology from the bucket chain excavators that first came on the scene early in the middle of the nineteenth century. Instead of an endless chain to support its digging buckets, the digging action of a BWE is provided by a rotating wheel fitted with buckets around its circumference and mounted at the end of a boom. Bucket wheel machines are usually connected to an elaborate system of conveyors, or a belt wagon (mobile conveyor), to transport the material considerable distances.

In 1908, British engineer A. R. Grossmith designed one of the first BWEs. It went to work uncovering ironstone in England. It was not a success, but it did pave the way for further development in England and Germany by several different companies. One of these was O&K\LMG, an established German manufacturer of bucket chain excavators who built their first bucket wheel in 1934. The following year, a machine with an output of 3,500 cubic yards per hour appeared.

A major breakthrough occurred in 1955 when O&K erected the first of the giant bucket wheel excavators at the vast open pit coal mine of Rheinische Braunkohlenwerke AG near Cologne, Germany. Billed as the largest mobile land machine in the world, this monster weighed 6,120 tons and could excavate more than 5,000 cubic yards per hour. Mounted on 18 crawler tracks, including its belt wagon, it was longer than two football fields. Over the next two decades this same mining company ordered many more monster bucket wheels, including the largest ever built. Size records for BWEs (based on operating weight) were broken in 1956 (8,200 tons); 1975 (13,400 tons); 1977 (14,500 tons); and 1991 (14,900 tons). The latter machine is the largest built to date. It can dig to the height of a 16-story building and has 18 8-yard buckets mounted on a wheel 71 feet in diameter. It moves overburden at rates of more than 300,000 cubic yards each working day, and its power comes from a multitude of electric motors totaling 18,700 horsepower.

In North America, geological conditions have limited the use of bucket wheel excavators, and thus mining operations using them are rare. BWEs are not suited to hard material, and boulders can wreak havoc with their delicate conveyor systems. As a result, few bucket wheel excavators have been manufactured in North America, but one notable exception is the United Electric Coal Companies (now Freeman United Coal Mining Company), which actually built its own machines. Six machines were built between 1944 and 1981 and successfully used at this company's mines in Illinois. Under the guidance of their president, Frank Kolbe, all were built on old stripping shovel bases, using four crawler assemblies, each with two crawler tracks to level and steer the machine. The resulting BWEs turned out to be five times as productive as the shovels they replaced!

The largest of the Kolbe "wheels," as they became known, was the W-4 built in 1959 with the enormous capability of 2 million cubic yards per month. The massive Kolbe W4 weighed 2,100 tons, carried a 27-foot-diameter digging wheel with 10 2-1/2-cubic yard buckets, and could tackle a face height more than 10 stories high.

German technology is responsible for the largest continuous excavators in the world, the giant bucket wheels. O&K built this example in 1991, which is that company's largest to date. Towering 30 stories high, it weighs in at 14,900 tons and operates at the Hambach Mine of Rheinbraun, Cologne, Germany. *Krupp Fordertechnik*

The discharge boom and wheel boom always remain in the same vertical plane as the Kolbe BWEs rotate from side to side during digging. A cross-pit BWE usually works in tandem with a stripping shovel. The shovel removes the lower, harder material, casting it into the adjacent worked-out pit where the coal has been removed. The BWE, with its superior reach, then removes the softer upper layer of the next cut, casting it on top of the material dumped by the shovel.

After the launch of the W4 in 1959, United Electric Coal announced the sale of the plans and patents for the Kolbe wheel to Bucyrus-Erie Company, which built several other machines of this type. The largest went to work in 1986 at the Captain Mine of Arch Coal Inc. in Illinois. Known as the 5872-WX, the excavator was mounted on the lower works of a Marion 5860, an 80-yard shovel. The 40-foot diameter wheel had 12 buckets of 2.14 cubic yards each. This immense excavator had an overall length of more than two football fields and an operating weight of 3,500 tons.

Although coal mining generally is on the increase, the type of coal found in the midwestern United States, including the Captain Mine where the 5872-WX worked, is unfortunately high in sulfur. Users of this coal now find difficulty in meeting the requirements of the Clean Air Act. Coal sales from this area have diminished, and the Captain Mine actually ceased production in 1998. The huge 5872-WX was sadly cut up for scrap in 1999.

Chapter 10

HYDRAULIC EXCAVATORS

In recent years, hydraulic excavators have probably become the most familiar of all earthmoving machines. They can be seen on every kind of construction job—from road maintenance, trenching, and foundation work to mass excavation on major industrial sites, as well as in quarries and surface mines. Today, these machines are made in all industrialized countries by hundreds of manufacturers all over the world.

Hydraulic excavators have generally replaced the old cable-operated excavator, except in the largest sizes. Compared with the cable excavator, they are cheaper to buy, are easier to operate, travel faster, and are more flexible in operation.

Although the backhoe and shovel fronts are used most on hydraulic excavators, there is a vast array of attachments available for all makes and sizes, to further increase the machine's usefulness. These include hydraulic clamshells, log grapples, rakes, rippers, shearers, packers, lifting hooks, and hydraulic hammers.

The first hydraulic shovels were used in the early 1900s and actually used water instead of oil in their hydraulic systems. They were not a success and were discontinued until technology advanced enough to use hydraulic oil systems. Today's hydraulic excavator has a relatively recent history, having been developed almost simultaneously in Italy, France, and the United States in the late 1940s. The early machines used low-pressure, unreliable hydraulic systems that were unable to withstand rigorous excavation. Hydraulic machines were thought by many to be just a passing phase. In fact, these early hydraulic excavators laid the foundation for what would become a complete revolution of the excavator industry.

The 1950s were pioneering years, when manufacturers gradually found solutions to engineering problems. The 1960s were developing years, when hydraulic excavators rapidly increased in size and many more manufacturers entered the field. The evolution of reliable hydraulic systems, using higher hydraulic pressures, increased the popularity of hydraulic excavators, and many of the staunch cable excavator manufacturers entered the

Liebherr's excavators have steadily increased in size over the years. Here a 994 belonging to Clay Colliery Company works in a British surface coal mine loading 100-ton trucks. It handles a 15-cubic-yard clamshell-type shovel bucket. *Keith Haddock*

A Caterpillar 5230 hydraulic shovel piles another load of rock on a hauler at a West Virginia surface coal mine. The clamshell-type shovel dipper allows loading of high-sided trucks without fear of the dipper door striking the truck body. The 5230 was launched in 1994 and is powered by a single Caterpillar diesel of 1,470 horsepower. *Eric C. Orlemann*

field. But their engineering was steeped in cable shovel design, and most found it extremely difficult to compete with their "hydraulics-only" counterparts in Europe and Japan. Some manufacturers made a brief entry and then abandoned hydraulics altogether. Also, North American manufacturers tended to employ low hydraulic pressures that didn't work well as excavators increased in size.

By 1970, hydraulic excavators had graduated into a major force in the excavating industry. That year Poclain introduced its EC-1000, a machine boasting a record-beating 10-cubic-yard bucket capacity. This machine was a milestone in excavator history. It not only demonstrated that hydraulic excavators were here to stay, but also proved that they could handle major tasks previously believed to be the sole domain of

cable machines. The cable excavator manufacturers viewed the larger hydraulic machines with apprehension. This was well founded because by 1980, O&K had launched its RH-300, a machine with a bucket capacity three times that of the Poclain EC-1000.

Currently, the hydraulic excavator industry is dominated by machines designed in Japan or Korea. Most of these are "construction-size" machines. The "mining-size" machines, the true giants of the industry found on large construction projects and in mining operations, are produced by just a few manufacturers. The world's largest hydraulic machines are German, namely O&K, Liebherr, and Demag, but competition comes from Caterpillar and P&H in the United States and Hitachi in Japan.

Harnischfeger (P&H), well known for its line of electric cable shovels, also offers mining-size hydraulic excavators. A Model 2250A shovel operates at the Cyprus Sierrita copper mine in Arizona. A 1,800-horsepower diesel engine powers the 372-ton machine. *P&H Mining Equipment*

Caterpillar unveiled its first hydraulic excavator, the Model 225, in 1972. This gained immediate acceptance and other models soon followed. Caterpillar unveiled its first "mining" shovel at the Las Vegas Minexpo show in 1992. The 5130 weighed in at 193 tons and was offered with buckets ranging from 11 to 14 yards. In 1994, the larger 5230 was announced, powered by a single Caterpillar diesel engine of 1,470 horsepower and buckets ranging from 18 to 22 cubic yards. These two excavators have since received weight increases and improvement upgrades.

P&H's first entry into the hydraulic excavator market was in 1964 when it acquired rights to a small excavator designed by Cabot

Corporation. From this machine, P&H developed the popular H312 and H418 which remained in production until 1976. From 1970 until 1974, P&H made certain hydraulic excavator models under license from Germany's O&K (for example, the 3-yard RH-25 shovel).

In 1979, using German technology, P&H designed and built in its Model 1200 hydraulic mining excavator. Weighing 177 tons and carrying 13-cubic-yard buckets, the 1200 was first in a line of hydraulic mining excavators that firmly landed P&H in the hydraulic heavyweight class. Since then, P&H has developed its hydraulic line upward to the present-day 1550 and 2250, with operating weights of 226 and 372 tons. These machines are available

When its 18-yard Model H241 came out in 1979, Demag demonstrated it was serious about big hydraulic excavators. The one shown here is in backhoe form and is loading 85-ton trucks for Miller Mining near Leeds, England, in 1986. *Keith Haddock*

The current largest machine from Hitachi is the colossal EX5500, announced in 1997. The 35-yard shovel has two Cummins engines developing a combined 1,250 horsepower. The first machine is shown ready to go to work for North American Construction at the tar sands operations near Fort McMurray, Alberta, Canada. *Wajax Industries*

A pair of Komatsu giants. This electric-powered Komatsu-Demag H485S hydraulic shovel loads a Komatsu Haulpak 930E truck at ASARCO's Ray Mine, Arizona. The shovel bucket holds 44 cubic yards, and it will take five passes to load the 320-ton truck. *Keith Haddock*

with electric power or a single diesel engine up to 1,800 horsepower.

Hitachi is one of a few Japanese manufacturers to challenge the "mining" excavator market and has certainly made its mark. Established in 1910, the parent company of Hitachi Construction Machinery Company Ltd. built it first excavator, an electric cable-operated mining shovel, in 1939. In 1965 Hitachi unveiled its first hydraulic excavator, the 3/8-yard UH03, the first to be developed using Japan's own excavator technology.

From this small beginning, Hitachi rapidly penetrated the world markets with its expanding excavator line, breaking into the mining excavator field in 1979 with the 10-yard UH801. It developed 800 horsepower from two Cummins diesels and weighed 173 tons. This machine, and the smaller 100-ton UH501 introduced in 1984, proved that Hitachi was a builder of reliable mining excavators. In 1987, the company launched its

This was the largest hydraulic excavator in the world when KMC Mining purchased it in 1995. The Demag H685SP works on overburden removal contracts at Syncrude's tar sands operation at Fort McMurray, Alberta, Canada. The 750-ton machine is powered by two Caterpillar diesels of 2,000 horsepower each. *Eric C. Orlemann*

Showing who's boss at the 1998 Bauma equipment show in Germany is this Liebherr 996 hydraulic shovel. The current top-of-the-line Liebherr carries a standard rock bucket of 36 cubic yards and tips the scales at 600 tons. *Francis Pierre*

EX-series consisting initially of the EX1000, EX1800, and EX3500, with standard shovels of 7, 15, and 30 cubic yards. The intermediate EX2500 was shown at the 1996 Las Vegas Minexpo as an 18-yard-class excavator with an operating weight of 263 tons. Hitachi's most recent mining excavator is the EX-5500, announced in 1997. This 35-yard shovel weighs 570 tons and carries two Cummins diesel engines providing 1,250 horsepower.

A builder of cable excavators since 1925, the long-established German firm of Demag built its first hydraulic machine in 1954. Known as the B504, it was the world's first all-hydraulic, crawler-mounted excavator to feature 360 degrees continuous swing. Through the 1960s, Demag rapidly replaced its cable excavators with hydraulic models of increasing size. The forerunner of today's giant Demag hydraulic excavators appeared in

1972 when Demag broke into the 100-ton-plus class with the H101. It carried a 6 1/2-yard shovel bucket and was powered by a pair of Caterpillar diesels that totaled 508 horsepower. More mining-size shovels and backhoes followed, including the 10-yard H111 in 1976 and the 18-yard H241 in 1978. The latter was Demag's first "super excavator," claiming the world's-largest title at 262 tons operating weight. This giant was powered by a single Cummins or GM diesel with more than 1,300 horsepower.

In 1986, the much larger Demag H485 went to work in Scotland for Coal Contractors Ltd., again capturing the world's-largest title for Demag. This machine was powered by a single MTU diesel engine of 2,500 horsepower, weighed 620 tons, and carried a 34-yard bucket. The current H485S version has been upgraded to a 44-yard capacity, weighs 690 tons, and has dual Cummins diesels—a massive 3,000 horsepower.

In 1995, contractor KMC Mining purchased an even larger machine from Demag to add to its vast equipment fleet working at Syncrude's tar sands operations in northern Alberta, Canada. Known as the H685 SP, it was at the time the largest and heaviest hydraulic excavator ever put in operation. The 750-ton machine is powered by two Caterpillar diesels of 2,000 horsepower each, and its bucket holds 46 cubic yards.

Even bigger is the Demag H740S, which went to work in 1999. Again purchased by KMC Mining for its tar sands operations, the new machine weighs 800 tons and carries a bucket of 52 cubic yards. Its two Caterpillar D3516B engines, each developing 2,200 horsepower, make it the most powerful hydraulic excavator in the world. Today Demag excavators are sold as Komatsu-Demag machines following a joint venture established between Demag and Japan's Komatsu Ltd. in 1996.

Liebherr entered the hydraulic excavator market in 1957 with the wheeled Model L-300.

Already well known for its tower cranes since 1949, Liebherr rapidly expanded its excavator line in the 1950s and 1960s. The company developed its 900-series excavators from the small R901 through to the R961, the largest in 1968 at 1 1/2-cubic-yards capacity. Since then, the top end of the line has pushed ever upward to serve the surface mining industry.

The 180-ton Model R991 was introduced in 1977 with a standard rock bucket of 10 cubic yards, and dual Cummins engines that total 720 horsepower. This machine was upgraded to the R994 in 1985 with a weight increase to 227 tons and a single Cummins diesel with 1,050 horsepower. The R996, introduced in 1995, currently spearheads Liebherr's drive for dominance in the world's mining excavator market. This monster machine weighs more than 600 tons and carries a standard shovel bucket of 36 cubic yards. Power is supplied by two Cummins engines with a combined output of 3,000 horsepower.

Another long-established German firm is Orenstein and Koppel (O&K). Founded in 1876, O&K built its first steam shovel in 1908 and soon established itself as one of the leading German excavator manufacturers. Their first hydraulic machine appeared in 1961 which was the RH-5, a small 1/2-yard machine. More than 20,000 were eventually sold.

Only 10 short years after its first hydraulic excavator, O&K launched the world's largest series-produced hydraulic excavator, the RH-60. This 124-ton machine was equipped with two Deutz diesel engines totaling 760 horsepower and an 8 1/2-cubic-yard capacity equipped as a shovel. Because this huge diesel-powered hydraulic excavator was a nimble machine, not dependent on a trailing power cable and easily dismantled to move in modular units, it was well received in the expanding surface coal mine industry. The RH-60 was followed by a larger machine, the RH-75 in 1976. Bucket size

O&K's first mining-size excavator was the RH-60, introduced in 1971. It was powered by two Deutz diesels totaling 760 horsepower. *O&K*

was increased to 10 cubic yards and weight to 150 tons.

O&K took a huge jump in size in 1979 and won the title to the world's largest hydraulic excavator. With an operating weight of 535 tons, and 34-yard bucket, the RH-300 easily surpassed everything built up to that time. The RH-300 was powered by two Cummins KTA2300C diesel engines, each producing 1,210 horsepower. The first unit was purchased by Northern Strip Mining Ltd. (NSM) to add to their large fleets of RH-60s and RH-75s in British surface coal mines.

Using the experience gained with the massive RH-300, O&K developed a series of successful giants. The 235-ton, 17-yard RH-120C was launched in 1983, followed by the 176-ton, 13-yard RH-90C 1986, and the RH-200, a crowd-puller at the Bauma equipment show in Germany in 1989. Somewhat lighter than the RH-300 at 512 tons, the RH-200 carries a similar-sized 34-yard bucket; but it

The O&K RH-300 was a monster machine when it came out in 1979, and it was the first to break the 30-cubic-yard barrier. The photo shows a maintenance man attending to the first RH-300, which was purchased by Northern Strip Mining Ltd. for use in its surface coal mines in England. *Dave Wootton*

The largest hydraulic excavator in the world today is this O&K RH-400. Developed jointly by O&K and Syncrude for the latter's tar sands operations at Fort McMurray, Alberta, Canada, the 900-ton shovel competes in a shovel-size class normally reserved for large electric cable shovels. *Eric C. Orlemann*

is a more efficient machine and is capable of greater output.

O&K's crowning excavator achievement is the RH-400, which went to work in 1997 at the Syncrude tar sands operation in northern Alberta, Canada. Again capturing a world's record for O&K, this 900-ton hydraulic shovel with 55-cubic-yard bucket and twin Cummins K2000E engines totaling 3,350 horsepower is ready to challenge any cable shovel. In late 1997, O&K's mining division, which includes the hydraulic excavators, was purchased by Terex Corporation.

The giant bucket of the first O&K RH-400 is giving these children a day to remember at O&K's Dortmund, Germany, plant. The 55-yard bucket, shown on the machine in the previous photo, is designed to load 240-ton trucks in three passes. *O&K*

G I A N T
DUMP TRUCKS

Hans Halberstadt

Acknowledgments

I am very grateful to three mine operators and three manufacturers, all of whom helped extensively with this book:

Kerr-McGee Coal Corporation, Jacob's Ranch Mine, Wyoming, where Mel Schafer played the role of tour guide and baby sitter.

Echo Bay Minerals Corporation, Battle Mountain, Nevada, Jeff Smith, Mine Superintendent.

Couer-Rochester, Lovelock, Nevada, Tim Maznek, Superintendent.

WISEDA LTD, Baxter Springs, Kansas, where Marilee Hunt, Administrative Services Manager, and Bill Lewis, VP for Engineering, both were generous with their help.

Komatsu Dresser Company, and Sales Support Manager for the Haulpak Division, Bill Bontemps, offered a wealth of support and insights.

Caterpillar, where export sales manager Pete Holman provided an articulate, detailed perspective on the virtues of mechanical drive.

I would also like to express my appreciation to the unsung heroes of the publishing world, the Motorbooks publishing personnel who help me have these adventures and then help clean up the mess afterwards: Tim Parker, Michael Dregni, Greg Field, Michael Dapper, Barbara Harold, Mary LaBarre, Bobbi Jones, Becky Allen, Jana Solberg, and Sharon Gorka. All these folks, in one way or another, are co-authors of my Motorbooks books, and I am grateful to each for their hard work and long hours—for which I, as the author, am unfairly credited.

Behind the Wheel

We were standing in the chill wind outside the headquarters for Kerr-McGee's huge coal mine about fifty miles south of Gillette, Wyoming, when this *thing*, a big, steel house with a wheel on each corner rolled across the parking lot. I had heard they were big, but I had no idea that anything that big could still roll around on tires.

That was my introduction to the marvelous and mostly invisible world of "mega" dump trucks. It was more than a pleasure—it was a privilege, too, because they don't go out in public; the only time anybody sees them is by invitation and at places like gold and coal mines, far from public roads.

These trucks can, when fully loaded, weigh in at almost a million pounds. They are far too big to be used on highways or roads, too tall to fit under bridges and highway overpasses, too heavy to run on concrete or asphalt without crushing the roadbed. Once you get over the super scale of the things, you see they *are* trucks, and are remarkably like conventional trucks with all the speed and agility of a regular pickup—and about 500 times more hauling capacity.

That first dump truck I saw was a Komatsu-Dresser Company Haulpak 830E, a $2.5 million vehicle that can carry more in a single trip than 500 conventional pick-up trucks. Similar ones are made by WISE-DA, Caterpillar, Unit Rig, and the VME division of Volvo, all offering the same kind of upscale efficiency for companies that have to move a LOT of dirt—or gold, silver, iron, phosphate ores, coal, taconite, or all sorts of other raw materials that come from the ground and go into the manufactured goods we buy.

I climbed aboard the Dresser 830 for an inspection. It is a long climb up to the cab, up a ladder like those found on ships. Inside, the cab is extremely conventional:

normal-looking dash, normal-looking wheel, Panasonic cassette player, business-like seats just like you'd find in any conventional truck. But these are very unconventional trucks indeed. From the cab you look down at the road, which is about 15ft below the cab. Remarkably, it drives like a regular truck, too.

Everything about them is big—size, fuel consumption (5gal to the mile), and the cost to buy, operate, and maintain. The sticker price for most 240 ton units begins at about $1,500,000 per truck—and that's for the stripped-down model; bed liners, fancy paint, fog lights, rock-guard fenders, oversized bed, and custom wheels are all extra. Dealer prep and transportation will run you about $25,000 alone. The sheet metal for the floor of the truck bed is 3/4in thick! A *single tire* costs $11,000. If a driver isn't careful, that tire can be destroyed in the first mile of travel. But any incident with these trucks is rare; they are too expensive to drive or maintain at anything less than a very high standard.

These mine haul trucks are so big that the only way to get them from the factory to the buyer is in pieces—lots of pieces. It takes about six semi-truck or railroad flat cars to transport the components of a large-capacity mine haul truck to the mine. Once all the pieces are on site, they are bolted and welded together. The truck will work all day, every day, for about ten years. By then it will have had many new sets of tires, several engine overhauls and replace-ments, and will have consumed about half a million gallons of diesel fuel. Then, when the warranty period (60,000 hours of operation for the WISEDA trucks) is used up and the when the frame is accumulating cracks and the bearings are becoming worn out, it may be time for the bone yard. But by then each truck will have moved a mountain's worth of material, all by itself.

They come in a range of sizes: *big, bigger, biggest*. The biggest of these off-high-way trucks are about 22ft high, 24ft wide, and 43ft long. With a full load in the bed, these weigh in at close to a million pounds, gross vehicle weight (GVW).

And they offer huge benefits to the mine owners. These big trucks actually *save* mine operators money because they can move more material at less cost than small-er vehicles. The result is that they normally operate twenty four hours a day, seven days a week, shuttling back and forth with their cargoes of dirt and coal and gold and silver.

The biggest will be rated to haul 250 tons—half a *million* pounds—of material at 35 mph. That 250 tons might include, for example, over $2,000 worth of gold, or enough coal to heat a whole neighborhood for an entire winter—and will typically move it for about 16 cents a ton. Every-thing about these trucks and the places where they work is BIG—the trucks, the mines, the economies, the importance of the work these things do. The result is smaller *unit* cost for each cubic yard of material they haul, and lower costs for things like electricity that are generated with the coal they carry. Actually, WISEDA has found some operators overloading these trucks up to 350 tons, but that reduces vehicle life, raises maintenence costs, and can void the warranty.

Even that 250 tons is less than the truck can actually manage; they cut back on the capacity a little to make them last longer. But when WISEDA was building their 240-ton truck, the engineers decided to see how much their new baby could *really* hold, and they filled one up with 270 tons of damp dirt and coal, just to see what would bend or break. Engineers are like that, and it is nice to know when they're loading you up with all that stuff, you aren't going to have the tires pop or the frame break while you're a comin' roun' the mountain.

These huge trucks save money by making each cubic yard or ton of material a little less expensive to move than in smaller trucks. For example, if a mine needs to move 15,000,000 tons of coal, ore, or overburden each year, a 120-ton capacity truck fleet will require *six* vehicles at a production cost of $4,065,000 per year. The big 240-ton-capacity trucks can haul the same fifteen million tons in the same time with just *three* vehicles and a production cost of only $3,000,000. That's over a million dollars saved by the mine operator.

Now, you'd think that a lot of experience behind the wheel of other big trucks would be a requirement for a job driving these things, but that's not the case. All of the mine operators I talked to agreed: *the best candidate for a driver of one of these things is someone who has never driven anything bigger than a pickup or a car.*

They've found that people coming out of other construction driving jobs have bad habits that can't easily be broken. They start the job thinking that they already know what to do. Novice drivers, on the other hand, tend to initially be terrified of the trucks—which is not such a bad idea, all things considered. They quickly get over the terror, become accustomed to the size and space of the vehicle, and rather rapidly are out cruising around the mine without any of the bad habits that might have been learned on semis, for example, or gravel trucks, or any of the large vehicles on the road today.

The training program for drivers is, in fact, the second amazing thing about the vehicles. Within the first week of training, a novice driver will be behind the wheel of a Dresser Company 830E or WESIDA 2450, and by the end of the second week, driving alone and earning a paycheck.

Chapter 1

A Short Course In Mining

Raw materials for all our food and manufactured products are either grown or mined. Most of our electrical power and all our natural gas and oil is mined. The costs for these products are kept low by efficient production.

There are two basic types of mining, "shaft" and "open pit." Of the two, the latter is by far the safest, fastest, and most economical. In early days, large open pits such as the famous Kennecott Copper Mines near Ely, Nevada, used railroad gondolas to haul large quantities of ore. The Copper Company built a railroad system in the pits and used dozens of locomotives and hundreds of gondolas to haul material to the crusher, the smelter, and the slag heap.

Opposite page, with the dump body elevated, the top of the lip of this Dresser 830E reaches as high as a window in the fifth story of a building. This truck is depositing overburden—dirt and rock—in the never-ending process of rearranging Wyoming.

But several economic developments have made railroad hauling impractical and prohibitively expensive. The productive life of an open pit mine is now about eight years, much too short a period to justify the time and expense of building a rail system. In addition, current conservation and reclamation practices require that the landscape be returned to its original contours and vegetation. Mine haul trucks have proven to be fast and flexible in removing and then replacing mined material.

As an example, most eastern US states use coal-fired electrical power stations. The coal comes mostly from huge deposits in the West, particularly from the Powder River Basin region south of Gillette, Wyoming, where a seam of clean, low-sulfur coal more than 50ft-thick runs for miles under the prairie. There are twenty five different coal mines in the Powder River area, and just one of them sends six entire train loads of coal east every day.

Above, a Dresser 630E. Pretty big, huh? You'd think so, but the big boy in the background isn't even the biggest at this mine; it is only the shrimpy little 190-ton Model 630E. Even so, those "monster" trucks from the car shows better run and hide from this or any other mine haul truck. Any of these could squish a "monster" truck flat—and many people wish they would!

Left, this cutaway drawing illustrates the typical powertrain layout: engine, cooling fan, and electrical controls forward, alternator amidships, and wheel motors housed within the wheel hubs. *Komatsu Dresser/Haulpak*

While the coal is clean and abundant, you don't get to just scoop it up; it is hidden below a layer of rock and dirt about 75-150ft thick—"over-burden" is what miners call it. While it is possible and sometimes practical to burrow through the overburden to reach the coal, a more efficient method uses open pits. Open pit mining begins with removal of the overburden, then the coal, and finally the overburden is replaced and reseeded in a

Above, a way to judge the immense height of a Dresser 630E wheel. Deb Hazlett is just over 5ft tall and tilts the scale at about 100lbs. She hadn't driven a truck or worked with heavy equipment previous to her employment by Kerr-McGee, but that's just fine. In fact, the best candidates for driving jobs with most mines are people without previous truck driving experience—and without the bad habits that come from that experience.

Opposite page, coal is one of the basic cargoes for the big off-highway trucks. This one has a special bed designed specifically for extremely large quantities of material. *Komatsu Dresser/Haulpak*

restoration phase. Within a few months the terrain looks virtually the same as before—although perhaps a bit lower—with the antelope and elk none the wiser.

The Jacobs Ranch Mine, operated by Kerr-McGee, is one of the big coal operations, sending six trains, each with over a hundred carloads, east every day. It has a reserve of 346,000,000 tons of coal under an overburden that is, on average, about 135ft thick. The coal contains less than a half-percent of sulfur and is only about six percent ash, making it a clean, very low pol-

luting energy source almost ideal for generating electricity. Each pound of this coal produces about 8,700BTUs for turning the turbines that drive the generators that produce the electricity for New York, Boston, Washington DC, and Richmond, Virginia.

Mines like the Jacobs Ranch (and there are twenty five in the Powder River Basin), and the gold and silver mines of Nevada, are fascinating places. Open pit mining is an amazingly clean and tidy process. Mine operators work alongside the Federal Bureau of Land Management (BLM) to assure that the environment is restored to its original contours. The miners remove the gold ore or the coal. Then, following BLM guidelines, they put everything back pretty much where it came from, with native vegetation species planted in the topsoil. In a short time it is virtually impossible to tell that this part of the land has surrendered any of its bounty. The pronghorns and elk are so abundant and so tame in their home on the range at Kerr-McGee's mine that trucks frequently have to wait for the animals to get out of the road.

Gold in Them Thar Hills

Compared to open pit coal mining, gold, silver, and other mineral mining is a

Opposite page, a Cat 789 coming at you. The 789 has been Cat's workhorse, a 190-ton mechanical drive truck that is probably the most popular Cat mine haul truck in the industry—in the world. You'll find them in Russia, Australia, and in many African and South American nations.

Above, standing on the edge of an open pit gold mine like this one, the Echo Bay mine near Battle Mountain, Nevada, it's hard to believe that mining only affects one-tenth of one percent of all Nevada's landscape. It is harder to believe—but true—that the productive life span of a mine like this is only about eleven years.

Above, there are quiet, comfortable accommodations for two in the spacious, air conditioned cab of this Dresser Haulpak truck. Stuff a cassette into the stereo—Willie Nelson's *On the Road Again* seems appropriate—and get out there and burn up the mine haul highway.

113

Above, these two trucks—a WISEDA 2450 (right) and a Cat 789—use quite different drivetrains to accomplish pretty much the same thing, although the Cat is smaller, at 195-ton capacity, than the WISEDA. Both are being served by a large Hitachi tracked shovel. Mine owners sometimes will run trucks with identical specs from different manufacturers side-by-side for years to test performance in "real world" conditions.

Below, pressure sensors in the suspension of this WISEDA 2450 measure the exact weight of the material in the truck; at a predetermined load, a system in the truck signals the shovel operator that it is time to go.

very different proposition. Gold in trace amounts is present almost everywhere, but in such small amounts that it is not practical to extract it from the rock in which it is dispersed. Chemical processes have been developed, however, that can efficiently remove even small amounts of gold and silver from large volumes of ore. Combine these processes with the efficiencies offered by large-scale pit mines and mine haul trucks, and ore that was once far too poor to get anyone's attention is now

Opposite page, the efficient operation of a modern mine depends on a carefully calculated interaction between several different kinds of technologies. Without a shovel to match its capacity, the big trucks would be just expensive curiosities. This massive P&H shovel scoops up the equivalent of 100 regular pickup truck loads in every "dipper" cycle. It takes three dipper cycles to fill each truck. *Komatsu Dresser/Haulpak*

Opposite page, loading operations are momentarily suspended while the welder makes repairs to the big 50 cubic yard shovel. The shovel is electrically operated, fed by a 4,160 volt/3-phase extension cord; during "dipper" operations, the system uses current on the up-stroke of the shovel, but it *generates* electricity as the shovel drops back down.

Below, this 190-ton capacity Dresser 630E has an aftermarket bed designed specifically for moving coal. It uses a tailgate and bed side extensions to provide greater volume capacity. Notice the relatively short wheel base; turning radius is only 80ft—not bad at all for a vehicle that is about four stories high and that carries as much as a hundred conventional pickup trucks!

yielding large quantities of mineral wealth.

Mining is one of Nevada's big businesses, even though mines occupy only a tenth of one percent of the state. Even so, each year Nevada produces over $2 *billion* worth of gold and silver—about 180,000 tons of gold and 575,000 tons of silver. Nevada produces 11 percent of the world's gold, and over 60 percent of US gold production.

Mining for gold, silver, taconite, coal, or barite is both simple and complicated. Once you know where the material is buried, the rest is pretty straight-forward.

It's a simple matter of: scooping away the waste material; putting it aside for a bit; collecting the coal, gold, or silver ore; then putting the waste material back in place. Complicating things are: the tremendous volumes of waste and ore; the need for efficiency and economy; and the tremendous scale of everything that happens. So while there's gold, silver, and coal just about anywhere you look, the only way you can profitably get at them is to be very, very

Above, part of Kerr-McGee's fleet of heavy Dressers wait patiently for their turn at the scoop. Notice the variety in bed size and configuration among these Dresser 630E and 830Es.

Left, one of the smaller shovels takes a quick maintenance break. That big reel on the right follows the shovel around; it keeps the extension cord tidy and out of the road. Behind the shovel is your electricity in the raw—clean, pure, low-sulfur coal destined for the power plants of the eastern United States.

119

Above, when the dump truck body tilts to discharge it's half a million pounds of gold and silver ore, the lip of the bed is about 45ft above the ground—about as high as a window in the fifth story of an apartment house or office building. This Dresser 630E is delivering ore to a crusher where the rocks will be pulverized, then processed to suck out the gold hidden within. The 630E is a mid-sized diesel-electric with a capacity of 135 cubic yards and a weight of about 170 tons. *Komatsu Dresser/Haulpak*

Opposite page, fifty yards and about 50 tons of material pour into the back of this big 830E. To protect the truck from such shocks, the bottom of the bed is steel plate 3/4in thick and the cab is protected by a canopy built into the body of the dump section. *Komatsu Dresser/Haulpak*

Above, it takes about ten cycles from this Cat 992 wheel loader to fill this Cat 776/777 truck, making each truck cycle far slower than the big 240-ton trucks when they are teamed with 50 yd^3 shovels that can fill the bigger trucks with only three to five dipper cycles.

Left, here's a Cat 789 truck at speed in a rare white paint job. One of these vehicles moving at speed is an awesome thought.

Above, most big mines fire a "shot" once a day, normally at a regular time. This shot was fired about a tenth of a second ago. Seven hundred and eighty seven charges, each containing about 300lbs of ammonium nitrate-fuel oil slurry, have just been initiated. The span from left to right in this photo is about 200yd.

Above, that stuff flying several hundred feet into the air is gold ore—several million dollars worth. But it is so diluted that you can't see any evidence of the gold in the ore, and special chemical processes are required to extract it. The little rocks visible are actually huge boulders flying through space. A sense of scale is provided by the two little vehicles on the far right side of the picture—those are both big Caterpillar dozers.

Above, wheel loaders like this Cat 992 wheel loader are mobile and flexible. Cat's line of wheel loaders for mine use range from 3 yd^3 to 13 yd^3. Here, it's loading a Cat 776/777 truck.

Above, a flock of WISEDA 240-ton "targets" await their turns at the shovel.

Above, one reason they don't send these trucks into town for a trip to the store is that the driver might have a little problem spotting grandma over in the slow lane. Visibility is *quite* restricted, as you can see from the deck of this Dresser 830E. Drivers learn to compensate, partly by becoming very proficient at judging the view in the wide-angle mirror.

efficient. If it weren't for these big trucks, and the savings they offer, mining some ore bodies just wouldn't pan out.

Operation of these mines is based on doing everything with maximum efficiency around the clock and calendar, and it's made possible by the large haul trucks like the Dresser 830Es. Even though the trucks cost millions of dollars each, cost about $120 an hour to run, and are worn out in about ten years, they permit mine operators to move a ton of ore, dirt, or coal for only about 16 cents—about one-third of what it used to cost with smaller, 32-ton trucks.

It's a Blast

You can't load the coal until you can get at it, and the best way to get at it is with explosives. Most of the waste material—the overburden—is too solid to permit the shovels to scoop it up, so it has to be loos-

Opposite page, Earl Hunter checks out the massive stern of the flagship of WISEDA's fleet, a WISEDA 2450. Although the basic layout of each of the 240-ton trucks is basically the same—two axles, dual tires on the back, about the same size, shape, and general conformance—note that WISEDA's rear end is a little less cluttered than other designs, and that the engine exhaust vents under the body near the pivot points rather than coming out of the bed support structure, as with other models.

Above, big trucks get big engines. This one is a V-16 model 396 from the German firm of MTU. Those sixteen cylinders each have a 6.3in bore and 7.1in stroke for a displacement of 63.3 liters, generating 2505hp. Red line is only 1900rpm. The engine alone weighs about the same as five passenger cars, over 11,000lb. MTU has sold 2,500 of these 396 engines, the world's most powerful currently in active service. MTU is now offering a new 595 series engine with 3,200hp for mine haul trucks—double the power of the engines that were considered the leading edge of technology only a few years ago. *MTU North America, Inc.*

Above, the Dresser 630E (slightly distorted here by the wide-angle lens) dwarfs Deb (who's up on the deck)—and everybody else, too. Those tires are 36x51 PRs. The truck is 39ft long and about 25ft high.

Opposite page, the mid-sized Cat 777 is a workhorse for the Couer-Rochester gold mine outside Lovelock, Nevada. That's because the 777, with its mechanical drive train and moderate capacity, fits the size and scale of the way this mine conducts operations.

ened, broken up, and pulverized. That's where the blasters come in. A major part of every mining operation involves the placement and detonation of massive amounts of explosives. Instead of high explosives like dynamite, these mines normally use a slurry composed of ammonium nitrate (a common fertilizer ingredient) and fuel oil. This mixture can only be detonated under certain conditions—it must be confined, and it takes something with the explosive intensity of a blasting cap to reliably prime it.

When it is time for a mine to start working a new "bench," the drilling crew will spend several days boring holes about 6in in diameter, about 35ft deep, 10ft apart over an area that may cover the size of several football fields. The result will be about

Above, another view of the 190-ton Cat 789 at speed. Cat has stayed with the mechanical-drive truck in spite of the claims and marketing successes of the electric-drive builders, and has its own version of just who is king of the lode. According to Cat, the title goes to its best-selling, fuel-efficient, mechanically reliable truck.

800 holes, each of which receives a charge of nitrate/oil slurry. These are then primed, the priming charges all connected to trunk lines, the trunk lines connected ultimately to a "hell box" (no longer the hand-held generator, today the hell box is a computer system).

Large mines will usually blast once a day, normally at a set time. As the scheduled blast time approaches, all vehicles and miners will be evacuated from the vicinity of the blast. Warnings are transmitted over the

Above, Earl checks the security of the fluid-fill panel on this WISEDA 2450. Although a sheet metal cover provides some protection from dirt and rocks, these critical components are checked for cleanliness and security before each shift.

radio. Supervisors count noses to confirm that everybody is out of danger. The master blaster presses the button, there are five short beeps from the hell box, a pause, then one long beep as the hundreds of blasting caps initiate their charges... and with exquisite slowness, a huge section of the mine rises up into the air. From half a mile away, what seem like small rocks can be seen soaring

into space—they are boulders, perhaps 10ft across. The sound of the shot echoes back and forth across the pit for twenty seconds or more, then dies away. Millions of pounds of rock and dirt and gold and silver are now fluffed up, softened, ready for the scoop, the mill, and the refinery.

"North road all clear," comes the radio report to the pit boss as the last of the dust settles.

"Ten-four. Pit Five to all personnel: channel one is clear. You may resume normal pit operations."

Everybody goes back to work. New

access roads are built first. Soon the huge electrical shovels roll up to the new work area. With the help of a few wheeled loaders to keep things tidy, they start to work on the material. The biggest shovel has a scoop that holds over fifty cubic yards of material. Three scoops will load the big 170-ton trucks, and five will load the biggest 240-ton WISEDAs and Dressers. The shovel works continuously, without pause, around the clock. The trucks slide back up into position to await their turn. Three "dipper loads" and each truck is full; with a beep, each rolls off to deliver the load. Without skipping a beat, the shovel turns to fill the truck on the other side while a

new truck slips into position where the first had been. In a few days, the entire area will have been worked, and the blasters will be ready for another shot.

The haul trucks deliver the overburden to a previously mined area, where it is deposited. After the overburden is removed, the coal is removed the same way, but delivered to a preparation plant for processing. At the Jacobs Ranch mine this is done at the rate of 4,000 tons per hour. The coal is loaded aboard rail cars and headed east within hours of being mined, and the overburden is back in place as part of the reclamation process that proceeds continuously.

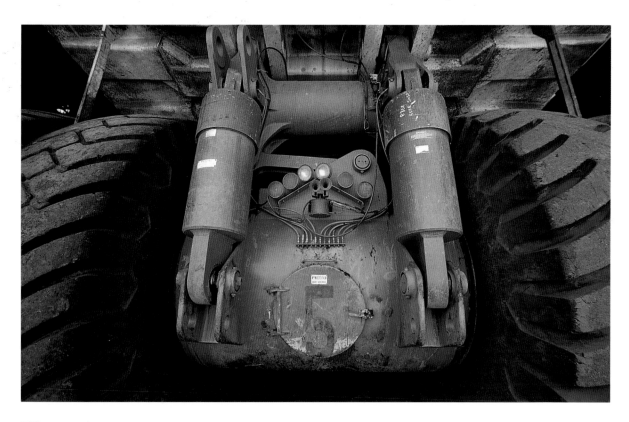

Opposite page, a Dresser 830E is in the shop for a little routine maintenance—well, actually, nothing about the truck is little, even the garage. That massive rear axle is about 5ft in diameter.

Above, the steering gear on this WISEDA 2450 isn't too different from any other truck or car, except in scale. The actual size of the engine seems far too small in proportion to the volume of the vehicle. The truck's tires are routinely chocked whenever the vehicle is parked.

Above, Oh, no! The differential is missing from this Dresser 830E!!! Actually, it was missing from the design of these electrical-drive trucks; there's enough empty space in the rear axle to climb in and take a nap—but the mechanics are far too busy and professional to do anything like that. The access panel allows inspection and maintenance of the huge GE 787 drive motors inside the wheel hub from the inboard side.

Above, just leaving the shovel, this big WISEDA 2450 has a full quota of payload. Although ore concentrations vary, there is between 10oz and 25oz of gold in this single truck load—a pound and a half mixed in with a half-million pounds of dirt and rock (and a fair amount of silver, too).

The trucks operate around the clock, in snow, ice, rain, and dust, and most are at fairly high altitude, at or above 5,000ft. They are driven about as fast as a regular pickup truck, about 30mph, even at three in the morning during a blizzard—with drop-offs from the side of the road unprotected by guardrails and with sheer drops of over 1,000ft.

Left, the driver—no shrimp himself—provides a scale to judge the massive 240-ton, a Dresser 830E.

Above, Cat isn't the only builder of large mechanical drive mine haul trucks painted yellow. This marvelous rendering provides an x-ray view of the major systems of this 95-ton truck, a Dresser 33M.

Opposite page bottom, you need a ladder to get into the engine compartment of a Dresser 830E, but there isn't a whole lot to be done once you get up there. One of the things that needs checking, though, are the connections for the ducting that feeds filtered air to the engine air intake. The mechanic provides some scale to judge the size of the cooling fan behind him.

Above, Earl Hunter inspects the engine oil level dipstick on a WISEDA 2450. The WISEDAs have their own built-in ladder to assist entry into the engine compartment. WISEDA offers three *basic* engines for the 2450: a Detroit Diesel V-16 149, a two-stroke-cycle with 1800-, 2000- or 2200hp; a Cummins KTTA-50C or K2000, both four-stroke engines with 1800 or 2000hp; a MTU V-12 396 four-stroke 1850hp. Other, much larger engines are also sometimes installed. MTU is currently offering a 3200hp diesel for use in these trucks—and in the next generation, a 300-plus ton capacity that may be coming down the road any day now.

Above, these huge Goodyear disc brake assemblies are mounted on the outboard portion of the wheel hub assembly. Inspection is easy— and a part of the daily routine.

Left, Earl Hunter, like all other drivers, performs a pre-shift vehicle inspection that is pretty much like a pilot's preflight inspection. Here Earl's checking the big Goodyear 40x57 tires on his WISEDA 2450. They last about 10,000 miles if they're driven carefully, about a mile if they aren't. A single wayward rock can destroy one, and on those extremely rare occasions when they blow, they blow *loud.* According to some tire makers, this is the biggest size that can be shipped by truck or rail to the mine site; tires appear to be the limiting factor preventing larger trucks.

Above, the Cat 777 is powered by a Caterpillar 8-cylinder diesel engine generating 920 gross horsepower at 1750rpm. That's about double the power of diesel engines used in eighteen-wheel semis out on the freeway. The engine uses twin turbos, is fed by a Cat fuel injection system, and has four valves per cylinder; the engine has a 6.7in bore, a 7.5in stroke.

Right, even the pistons in million-dollar engines fail eventually. The skirt section of this one has separated at the lower ring. Such failures are rare—and to be anticipated from engines that run about twenty-two hours a day, seven days a week, for years on end.

Above, another view of Deb's rig, the Dresser 630E, at speed. The 630E is Dresser's 190-200 ton class vehicle with an empty weight of 283,000lb and a MGVW of 685,000lb, only about 150,000lb less than the 630's bigger brother, the 830. Truck 26 has a bed extension that increases the volume capacity of the truck for lighter materials, although the weight restrictions still apply.

Right, even though the engines are huge, the components are not much larger than you'll find in more conventional vehicles—and, as with conventional engines, valves need routine attention.

Above, every one of these trucks is, in a way, a custom vehicle. No, they don't get mag wheels and candy apple paint jobs, but each buyer normally demands a different set of specifications in exchange for their $2.5 million; this one has an unusual ladder arrangement that ought to make it a collector's vehicle someday. *Komatsu Dresser/Haulpak*

Left, notice that Cat 789's rear axle is much smaller than the equivalent electric drive vehicles, and the beefy suspension elements and bed supports. Also visible are the pivot points for the bed and the exhaust outlets; the heat of the exhaust is used to warm the bed of the dump section to keep the load from sticking during extreme cold weather.

Above, Deb Hazlett scurries up the ladder to the cab of her Dresser 630E.

Left, here's what they look like when they're new, all clean and pretty. But this truck works for a living, around the clock, and will soon be spattered with mud, dinged by flying rocks, smudged by exhaust. It should be good for about ten years of continuous service, about 80,000 hours of operation. That little thing at the bottom of the ladder is the driver, not a little kid with a mustache. *Komatsu Dresser/Haulpak*

Chapter 2

A Short History of Tall Trucks

The design of these trucks is a response to many conditions and criteria. Mines traditionally have been extremely dangerous, dirty, stressful places for people to work. But, like so many other things in mining, these trucks were designed with the motto, "safety first."

The trucks operate around the clock, in snow, ice, rain, and dust, and most are at fairly high altitude, at or above 5,000ft. They are driven about as fast as a regular pickup truck, about 30mph, even at three in the morning during a blizzard—with drop-offs from the side of the road unprotected by guardrails and with sheer drops of over 1,000ft. All these conditions might make for a dangerous work place, but

Opposite page, the traditional layout for dump trucks, six wheels with two forward and four in back, has proved to be the best solution to the problem that anybody has come up with so far. But each of those massive tires costs from $11,000 on up and will last about 40-60,000 miles or less. *Komatsu Dresser/Haulpak*

many features and procedures have been developed to make truck driving in the mines a relatively low-stress, satisfying, and safe occupation.

The first big modern-design trucks designed for use in open pit mines were developed in the late fifties (Haulpak Company claims the first, a mechanical drive, built in 1957) and early sixties (Unit Rig & Equipment Co. made the first diesel-electric drive in 1962). These were mechanical drive vehicles, with conventional engine and powertrain systems much like any other truck on the road, with capacities of 20 or 30 tons at first, growing rapidly to 65 tons within a few years. The mechanical drivetrain—diesel engine, torque converter, mechanical transmission, differential—turned out to be the limiting factor for the vehicles. As the components got bigger, so did the maintenance costs, and the weak link seemed to be the transmission.

The truck designers of that era adapted

Above, despite the size of these trucks, mine traffic is *fast*. The trucks turn laps, rather like race cars; the speeds are only in the 30 to 35mph range, but that is plenty fast for the grand prix de Wyoming where the gold medal is in the back of every truck, a new one on every lap—production, efficiency, profitability, lower prices for consumers. One of the ways drivers are evaluated is on how many laps they turn in a shift. A Dresser 630E is shown barreling along here.

the same basic technology used in diesel locomotives: a large engine coupled to an electrical generator instead of a transmission, the generator, in turn, wired to powerful wheel motors. The first of the breed

were introduced in 1963, with a capacity of 85 tons, and just two years later the first 100-ton capacity truck hit the road. The result for mine operators was a sudden and dramatic decrease in maintenance costs and a huge increase in truck availability.

It was obvious that increased capacity meant higher efficiency, but it took time to figure out how to make these trucks even larger. By the late sixties their capacity had grown to 120 tons, then to 150 tons by 1970. About twenty years ago the first 170 ton diesel-electric truck was introduced; WISEDA built the first 200+ton diesel elec-

Above, this Dresser 630E is taking on a load of overburden, the simple dirt that covers the Powder River Basin coal deposit to an average depth of about 75ft. When the shovel operator decides, based on experience and judgment, that it is time to go, one blast on the shovel's air horn will send the driver off on another trip across the bench.

tric rear dump hauler in 1982, and today the standard of the industry is the 240ton truck. And although the diesel-electric technology has come to dominate the market, Caterpillar today sells a 240-ton capacity truck with a mechanical drivetrain.

Those 170-ton trucks have turned out to be the workhorses of the open mine industry, and can be seen zipping around most coal, gold, silver, and other mines in the US, Canada, and elsewhere around the world. But, as big as they were, they *still* weren't quite big enough for some mine operators, and 200-ton designs were built and tested as far back as 1970. These early "mega trucks" used power packs and drivetrain technologies borrowed directly from railroad locomotives—and they didn't work out. The diesel engines had the horsepower but were designed for low RPMs and were extremely heavy. The electrical drive motors were also exceedingly heavy and didn't match the requirements of a truck, even one on steroids.

There are four essentials to building any successful vehicle: chassis, drivetrain, tires, and powerplant. For these big trucks, the critical component became a diesel engine with sufficient power—2,000-2,500hp for the biggest models today—*and* relatively high RPMs and throttle response.

Dead weight on a mine haul truck costs about $2 per pound per year, so the chassis needs to be a compromise between strength and light weight. Originally, mine trucks were built according to the "one pound of truck equals one pound of payload" theory, although the new ones are about 1.4lb of payload to each pound of truck. Light weight reduces stress on the tires and allows the trucks to climb the fairly steep grades found in pit mines.

The general layout for these trucks is approximately the same, regardless of man-

Below, while the Dresser 630E maneuvers into position at the shovel, a "blade" attends to the housekeeping chores, cleaning up spills and keeping the haul road clean and neat.

Above, Kerr-McGee's Dresser 630E Number 2026 is powered by an 1800hp turbocharged diesel engine driving a GE GTA-22 alternator connected to two GE 788 wheel motors. Dresser and WISEDA both claim that electric-drive technology is, when you get to the bottom line, the most economical method. Caterpillar, though, has stuck with mechanical-drivetrain technology—for which it also makes a strong claim for high efficiency.

ufacturer. The chassis is designed so that the weight is distributed about equally on the front and rear tires when empty (there are normally two wheels forward and four wheels aft); loaded weight distribution shifts about two-thirds to the back axle, one-third on the front, all in an effort to load all tires equally.

Frame and Suspension

The frame is built up from sheet nickel-copper (WISEDA uses A710 alloy steel, a particularly costly but tough and flexible formulation, and other builders use similar alloys), welded together in what the builders call a "donut" or "horse-collar" frame, with tubular cross-members. This particular type of alloy resists cracking when cold, a problem with other materials and a cause for the failure of some earlier designs. The frames from all builders tend to be somewhat wedge-shaped when viewed from the side, with lots of material in the rear to support the loaded bed. The "horse collar" surrounds the engine, adding stiffness to the front end of the structure.

The frame is an extremely critical part of these vehicles, even more critical than those of cars or conventional trucks because of the loads and stresses placed on these haulers. The manufacturers have all pretty much converted to using computer-aided-design (CAD) and -manufacturing (CAM), and you can see why. One of the builders, Dresser Company, also puts the frames and other major components through a testing program that flexes and stresses these components in a lab environment, looking for weaknesses in design and construction before the trucks are shipped.

One novel feature of these big trucks has been the use of engine exhaust gasses to heat the vehicle dump body, making the steel alloy less susceptible to cracking on frigid Nevada and Wyoming winter nights and to keep the load from freezing to the bed of the truck. The exhaust is ducted into the frame from the engine, then vented at the back; designers, though, are moving away from this system because the exhaust

gases erode the metal passages over time.

Another novel feature is that the engines, and many of the other components, are designed for relatively easy removal and replacement. The engine usually is mounted on rails that allow the power pack to slide forward, out of the truck, for easy access and major maintenance. For smaller chores, though, a ladder is required because the upper portion of the engine is about 10ft off the ground.

The suspension systems are somewhat similar to those of conventional vehicles, hydro-pneumatic designs, but much larger and with some modifications. Good handling and ride are just as important in a mine truck as any other professionally driven vehicle. Instead of gas/oil shocks, some trucks use solid rubber components to replace shock absorbers and springs. The huge rear axle is actually a tube that supports the rear drive motors and wheel hubs. The rear axle is attached to the body with drag links and "elastometer" rubber suspension elements that transmit the load from the frame to the wheels.

The front wheels and steering gear aren't too different from those on smaller vehicles. While the specs vary a bit from one make and model to another, a typical 240-ton WISEDA truck's front end has 1 degree of camber, 8 degrees of king pin inclination, and 4 degrees of caster angle; the result of this design is that the vehicle has a tendency to return to a straight-ahead direction. This WISEDA design's wheels maintain their positive camber as they move vertically. Steering forces tend to self-cancel. The result is a vehicle that minimizes wear on the tires and the driver.

Some trucks use massive versions of conventional nitrogen gas-over-oil shock absorbers while older WISEDA models employ a Firestone product called a "marshmallow," a rubber cushion and guide assembly that appeared to do the same thing with no moving parts at a lower initial cost and with minimal maintenance; WISEDA stopped using the product recently though because it turned out to be less economical in the field than nitrogen/oil shocks. The front wheels have a full 12in of vertical travel. These front wheels themselves rotate dual roller bearings fitted to axle spindles that are up to 18in in diameter.

Drivetrain—diesel-electric

As noted, the idea behind the diesel/electric trucks is essentially the same as that used on railroad locomotives: A very powerful diesel locomotive drives a generator, and the generator's output powers large, geared-down, DC motors at the wheels.

The GE 787 motors are geared down through a planetary gear system, normally at about a 28.8:1 ratio (although higher and lower ratios are available, depending on builder and on buyer). The current to drive these motors is controlled through a large power management system located next to the driver's cab.

Above, this ore body was once mined with traditional methods of shafts and tunnels; the rusty rails that once guided ore cars deep below ground are now exposed to daylight for the first time in many decades. While the scoop and truck work the bench, the drilling crews are busy on a shelf several hundred feet up the pit. *Komatsu Dresser/Haulpak*

When the driver steps on the accelerator, an electronic signal to the engine electronic governor causes the diesel engine to speed up, and that drives the alternator. Electronic controls, regulated by the retard and throttle pedal which each operate a potentiometer cause the engine to speed up. Engine speed is controlled by power demand. With the new GE Statex III system, the micro-processor controller for the drive system looks at power demand and cuts back on engine speed if full horsepower is not required. Direct current is generated, and a set of "power contractors" in the electrical power management

Above, finally, a turn at the shovel for this Dresser 630E. It takes about three 50 cubic yard dipper cycles to fill this 630 to capacity. The shovel operator and the truck drivers never miss a beat; while one truck is being loaded on one side, an empty truck is backing into position on the other. As soon as one is filled it drives away and the shovel starts servicing the other truck, without a break in the tempo.

system are engaged. Current flows to the wheel motors through thick cables about 2in in diameter, and the current turns the motor. It is an elegant system with a minimum of parts—although all the parts are large ones.

Drivetrain—Mechanical

Smaller trucks from Dresser Company and everything from Cat use a drivetrain based on a variation of the traditional mechanical drivetrain. Cat's 789 starts with a big 1800hp engine coupled to a Caterpillar-designed and -manufactured twin disc torque converter, and a driveshaft that feeds into a planetary power shift transmission. Cat's automatic transmission is electronically controlled and executes shifts up or down based on factory pre-sets that are designed to make the vehicle more efficient than traditional hydraulic-mechanical designs. The planetary power shift transmission and final drive deliver the torque to the wheels. While this is a more complex system than the diesel-electric set-up, it manages to convert more fuel into haul-miles, and Cat emphasizes those savings. The competition, however, claims the mechanical drive costs more to maintain and that incremental improvement in electric drive control systems have negated fuel savings of mechanical drive.

The electric vs. mechanical controveryis an ongoing question in the industry. Recent tests at the Echo Bay mine showed that the diesel-electric WISEDA truck achieved more ton-miles per gallon than the Cat 789B and that, overall, WISEDA trucks were more efficient—while other tests with other electric drive manufacturer's trucks seemed to allude to achieving marginally opposite results.

Wheels, Tires, and Brakes

Most (not all) of the big haul trucks use the same basic layout, with two wheels forward and duals astern, all the same massive size. The wheel rims alone are typically 57in in diameter and 29in in width on the 240-ton class trucks; that means the tires are each about 12ft in diameter and weigh about 4 tons apiece.

Those tires are the second-largest cost for operators of these big trucks, right after fuel. Standard for the big 220- and 240-ton vehicles is the 40x57 size (in your choice of bias or radial ply), mounted on 29x57 rims.

At $15,000 to $16,000 and up for a tire, it pays to be very careful about them, so drivers are taught to drive smoothly and to avoid running over rocks in the roadway—a common hazard and one that can destroy a brand new tire.

When a tire does blow, everybody knows about it; they are *loud*. And although an unlikely occurance, if it happens while the truck is bopping around a corner at speed or gets up on a berm, with a full load and a high center of gravity (CG), it is quite possible that the whole rig will roll over on its side like an elephant that has tripped and fallen. Tires last for about 40,000 to 60,000 miles in normal service, although a careless driver can destroy one in the first mile. Tires turn out to be the limiting factor on these vehicles—the 40 x 57 size being the biggest currently built that can be shipped by road or rail.

The oversized nature of these trucks provides the brake designers with a megasized headache. The trucks operate at the same speeds as smaller vehicles on construction sites—around 20-30mph—but with a GVW approaching a million pounds, the inertia... well, your dinky little drum-and-shoe brakes just aren't going to stop it.

There are two basic kinds of brakes available to the driver, each operated by its own pedal. The first is what is called a "dynamic" retarder system, a way to slow the truck on grades and when preparing to stop; this turns the wheel motors into generators and instead of using current, they convert wheel motion to electrical power. Although other types of vehicles use this concept and store the resulting power for later use, the trucks convert the current into heat, rather like a huge, mobile toaster, through a bank of resistor grids (on the right side of the cab deck on the WISEDAs) exposed to the air. A high-speed blower provides cooling air flow, otherwise the resistor grid would quickly melt. This dynamic retarder system works best in the slow speed ranges of about 7-17mph.

But the retarder doesn't stop the vehicle, it just slows it and converts inertia to heat. To completely stop the vehicle still requires mechanical brakes—the biggest set of disc brakes anywhere. Again, these are quite like those on cars and conventional trucks, scaled up many times. Usually this involves a big disc revolving at wheel speed instead of drive-motor armature speed; both work and both have virtues. A wheel rotor turns at far slower RPMs, has a far larger disc, and has become the preferred type. The disc and associated calipers are mounted on the outboard side of the wheels where they are quite easy to inspect and service. WISEDA tested the brakes on the 2450 by driving it at 20mph down a minus-6 degree slope; with a 240-ton load, the vehicle came to a full stop in 135ft. Society of Automotive Engineers (SAE) and Canadian braking codes require trucks to successfully perform a series of complete full-brake stops with less than fifteen minutes between stops within a speci-

fied distance. For the WISEDA KL-2450 that test involved a 250 ton load, 22mph road speed, brought to a full stop in less than 120ft.

The GE 787 Drive System

The 170-ton capacity design appeared to be the practical upper limit for these vehicles until around 1980, when General Electric developed a more efficient drive motor system, their model 787. This is really a rather fiendish design; the motor actually becomes part of the wheel assembly itself, resulting in a complete system that integrates the motor, reduction gear, wheel, and tire. The 787 is a huge motor, almost 6ft in diameter. This size is actually an advantage, offering structural stiffness and strength advantages over motors with smaller dimensions.

Servicing these motors is surprisingly simple—if you've got the tools. The essential components are inside the rear wheel hub assemblies, so all you have to do to get at the brushes, brakes, and planetary gears that drive the truck is to pop off the rear hub and there it all is, ready for your attention.

Gear ratios vary. The big WISEDA comes with a 28:1 standard, but other builders use 32:1. It really depends on the kind of mine conditions where the truck will be working. A low ratio offers higher speed on flat road segments while a higher ratio makes hill climbing with a full truck easier.

One of the main reasons for putting a speed limiter on the vehicle isn't because the young drivers would be out doing "wheelies" in the dirt, or drag racing in them, but because the armatures and the tires are so big that centrifugal forces could tear them both apart. Excess speed causes heat build-up in the tires, too, and that can cause tread seperation and tire failure. That's why General Electric puts a 2400rpm limit on the drive motor armature; at that speed (about 33-35mph) power is automatically cut out and the dynamic retarder is engaged.

Power Packs and Cooling

There have been several limiting factors for the size of mine haul dump trucks over the years, and power packs were certainly an early one. Initially, locomotive engines were tried, but they were designed for a completely different kind of operating environment. What was needed was something with the power to push a million-pound vehicle up a grade, that was reasonably responsive, and that offered practical fuel economy. The massive weight of the locomotive engines was one of the critical problems of the early trucks.

Until the early eighties, the largest engine for truck use was 1600hp and that just wasn't sufficient for the operating conditions found in the mines. But since then came 1800hp, 2000hp, and now 2500hp and 3200hp diesels to drive the alternator and provide more than enough power, responsiveness, and fuel economy to make the big trucks very efficient.

The big 2500hp diesels are used in the biggest trucks, but not all that go-power is available. The builders sometimes limit available horsepower to about 2000hp to improve economy and durability of these big, expensive engines, but other models may use the full engine output. Engine speed governors are installed on virtually all off-highway trucks to limit top speed to about 35mph; they could go a lot faster but the hazards from driver error and mechanical failure become prohibitive.

These engines are all turbocharged and fuel-injected diesels, usually in V-16 designs, but some in a V-20 format. These immense engines all have a very high power to weight ratio, and they come from a variety of manufacturers, based on the customer's preference; Cummins, Detroit Diesel, Caterpillar, and the German firm of MTU all contribute engines to the breed.

The cooling system uses a removable-tube radiator and large, low-speed fan combination for maximum efficiency. On the big WISEDA 2450, this fan is about 7ft across and spins at only 690rpm. So what? Well, that low speed reduces parasitic power loss from the cooling system to just 50hp—only about 5 percent of the engine output, and a lot less than the old, smaller, high speed fan previously used on earlier designs that consumed about 10 percent of engine output. Total parasitic loss varies with model and manufacturer but on the WISEDA the fan, air compressor, pumps, air conditioner, and battery-charging system account for about 90hp total.

The Dump Body and Hydraulic System

The dump body looks like a simple design problem but is actually another place where truck designers fuss and fume with each other about what constitutes "best." All are extremely beefy; the steel plate for the floor is about 3/4in thick, the sides are made of about 3/8in plate.

The body of the dump section is formed into a large box that places the load relatively low, with the center of gravity carefully calculated to keep the vehicle from being any more top heavy than it already is. But when the driver backs into the berm to unload that half-million pounds of ore or overburden, it all needs to slide right out when and where it belongs. Since sometimes this material is wet, or frozen, and perhaps quite sticky, this is also part of the designer's concern.

To deal with these problems, the beds are typically broad, flat, vee-shaped spaces. Loaded, the material is carried low. When the big hydraulic rams are actuated, there is nothing to hang up the dirt, rocks, and gold nuggets and they pour out on command. On Cat trucks the floor slopes forward at a 7.5degree angle, shifting the load forward and down as it is dumped in by the shovel. Cat also uses a V-shaped bottom to the body.

The dump bed is raised by a two-or three-stage cylinder—a 13in first stage and a 9in second stage—pressurized by an approximatly 2400psi hydraulic system powered by a pump driven from the engine accessory section. The bed tilts to about 50degrees, the extended lip (which protects the cab from wayward rocks) will top out about 45ft above the ground.

On the left side of the driver's seat is a lever that controls the dump portion of the body. This control has four positions: RAISE, HOLD, FLOAT, and LOWER. When you back into your "drift," you set the hand brake, shift to neutral, pull up on the lever to the raise position. Hold it there while the bed comes up and all that gold ore pours out into the crushing mill. You can speed up the process by raising engine rpm, but it still takes about 20 seconds for the bed to come to the full-up position. At any time during the raise cycle the driver can stop the extension by lowering the control lever slightly to the HOLD position.

Once the load has been delivered, the control lever is lowered to the full down position, the LOWER position; the bed will cycle back down into position in about 9 to 15 seconds. The FLOAT position is the lowest control lever position and the appropriate position for normal, underway operations.

The Cab

The operator's cab in these trucks is a little armored cubicle framed in heavy steel beams. That's because almost any accident, including the equivalent of a fender-bender at low speed, will be extremely dangerous. Mine operations have a rich potential for hazard: trucks can roll over (although that's

Above, here's another view of the Cat 992 wheel loader in action. This is Cat's biggest wheel loader; it's design includes a Z-bar linkage that permits tremendous leverage to the bucket, essential for the loader to quickly break material out and deliver it to the truck, which, in this case, is a Cat 776/777.

extremely rare); skid out of control on slick, steep grades; trucks can collide with other vehicles; and (perhaps worst) go over the side of the pit and tumble to the bottom. While the safety record of these vehicles and their drivers is excellent, the designers try to take minimal chances.

But when you climb aboard and slide in behind the wheel, all that attention to safety is invisible. Your throne is completely adjustable up and down, fore and aft. The cab is not just air conditioned, it is pressurized to keep dust out, even when you open the door. It is soundproofed, too, filtering out most of the crashes and roars going on outside.

Instrumentation varies from one builder to the next, but all use extremely high-quality components in the dash. One manufacturer (Dresser Company) uses elaborate and expensive liquid crystal displays and touch-sensitive screens. The result looks like something from an F-15E Strike Eagle; the indicated airspeed will be lower but the basic idea is the same. Others use more conventional instrumentation.

The steering wheel is adjustable, too, for tilt and reach. All the controls are designed to be arrayed logically and comfortably, and most are adjustable to suit the full range of operators.

Above, this 240-ton capacity Dresser 830E truck is equipped with the factory standard equipment dump body, good for moving about 170 cubic yards of material. After its turn as a target for dipper, it will lumber off to unload on the far side of the mine pit. Dump angle is 45deg and the height of the bed lip during the dump is 44ft.

'Like Driving Your House Down the Street from an Upstairs Window'

Debbie Zimmerman is just over 5ft tall and weighs in at about 100lb. Like many other drivers of mine haul trucks, she hadn't driven anything much larger than a cowboy-style pickup before she came to work for Kerr-McGee's Jacob's Ranch Mine. You'd think that such inexperience would be a handicap for a fledgling driver, but as noted earlier, that's not the case. Fleet owners and trainers all pretty much agree that you need to start working with these trucks without a lot of bad habits developed from operating other, smaller trucks and vehicles. The best drivers seem to be people who show up with an open mind and a willingness to learn.

"All this was brand new to me," Debbie Zimmerman says of her introduction to the profession of mine haul truck driver. "I had no experience with driving or construction, so everything was somewhat overwhelming—the size, the noise, the tires that were taller than your head, the shovels, the track dozers—everything was just huge. But you ride around with a driver for a while, then they let you drive the vehicle while they ride along to make sure you know what you're doing, that you are safe. Then you are on your own.

"You are scared to death," Debbie says with a laugh of that first time behind the wheel. "I was really nervous. But you get over that quickly—they teach you what to do, show you what to look for, and the help of the other drivers who've been here for years gets you through. The first time I was a *little* panicked, but when the time came to actually drive, you go slowly at first. It was hard to judge distances at first; you can't see what's happening over on the far side of the truck, but you learn to know where the tires are, how to back into the dozer, to pull into the shovel, to look out for rocks. But basically, it is just like driving a car—a car that is two stories high!

"After you are on your own for a while and you notice that you are getting into the shovel correctly, into the dump position correctly, you get an enormous feeling of confidence. This happens after only two or three weeks of driving on your own—you know the basics and you are doing these well. Of course you know you've got much more to learn.

"You have to be very aware of what is going on around you, all the time—the other people on the ground, the vehicles moving around you."

Debbie, like every other driver, starts her shift by getting a bus ride to the truck she shares with three other drivers. In her case, that will be at around midnight, because by preference she works the graveyard shift from midnight until 8 in the morning.

The truck will be chocked and the engine will be shut down, but still warm from the swing shift. It will have been fueled earlier in the day; the 1,000gal tank will last for 24 hours of normal operation. Debbie, like all drivers, inspects the vehicle before she accepts it by conducting a "pre-shift inspection." This is very much like a pilot's preflight inspection, a slow, ritualistic walk around the vehicle looking for anything that might be a hazard to safe operation: cracks in the frame (particularly in the "nose cone" area); all the hinge pins are in place; the rims are secure; no cuts in the tires; no leaks from the hydraulic or fuel lines; no broken or dirty headlights; or any other system that may have failed during the last shift. Then she pulls the chocks from the wheels, stows them in their racks, and climbs up the long ladder to the flight deck of the big Dresser Company 830E Haulpak, climbs into the cockpit, and straps in.

"I adjust the seat—*real important for me*—" says Debbie, who's only 5ft 1in, "and make sure the windows are clean. I adjust the mirrors, honk the horn once as a warning, then I start the engine." Engine starting is, for the driver, just like starting a car; you turn the key to the start position, hold it until the big diesel fires, then release it to its spring-loaded RUN position.

The instrumentation is familiar to anybody who has driven a car, although it is a little more complete. Everything is pretty obvious—and of the highest quality: digital tach and speedometer; engine oil pressure, coolant temperature, air pressure, electrical output, fuel quantity. The ignition switch is labeled MASTER SWITCH, and is over on the upper left side of the panel; the key will be in it when the driver takes over the vehicle. In the same part of the panel, right where the driver can easily monitor them, are some of the warning system lights: control air, body up, retard control, lube pressure. On the right side are more warning lights: engine fault, engine check, electrical fault, warm air flow, ground fault, steering pressure, and brake pressure. There are also controls for the retard regulator, the parking brake, head lights, dash lights. Overhead will be the engine hour meter, breaker panel, and a vacuum system control—along with an absolute essential for all truck drivers everywhere, the stereo sound system.

The steering wheel looks like any other, and below, right where they belong, are the three pedals we all know and love—except that two of the three are nothing like their automotive counterparts. The center pedal, the one where the brake goes in a car or conventional truck, is the retarder control; you apply it to slow the vehicle when descending a grade or coming to a stop. The far left pedal, the one that ought to be a clutch, operates the disc brakes; but you use those sparingly, at low speed. The rotors are almost 4ft in diameter and could rapidly heat up to a bright, glowing red if they were to be used indiscriminately.

"It starts just like a car," Debbie says, "and it will usually fire right up. It has a high-idle switch that kicks it up to 1600rpm for a few moments while the air pressure and hydraulic pressure come up." Then the parking brake is released, the gear lever advanced to FORWARD and off she goes for another day in the coal mines.

Mine traffic is almost invariably on the left, British-style. The rationale for that is that, in the unlikely event of two fully loaded haul trucks having a head-on collision (it hasn't ever happened), the chances of the drivers being in the middle of the mix-up are lower; they will tend to be on the outside of the massive ball of twisted wreckage instead of at its center. "If a collision should ever happen," Debbie says, "you will be off-side to off-side, rather than cab-to-cab. This should make it more likely that the drivers will not be directly involved.

"Learning to back into the shovel is very hard to learn. Every shovel operator has a set of peculiarities and preferences, and we have to learn what they are. Some want you to back in quickly, another will want you at a tighter angle, or closer than another, and you learn that by working with that operator." Ideally, the shovel operator never misses a beat; there is always a fresh truck waiting in position on the off side when another truck is loaded and departs. That kind of efficiency only happens when the shovel operator and the truck drivers are fully proficient and are playing on the same team. It is a pretty thing to watch—trucks slide into their positions alongside the vast shovel, are loaded, and depart as fresh trucks arrive in a massive, mechanical ballet.

"*Everybody* works together here," Debbie says. "If there is a problem—a truck blows a tire, for example—everybody knows what to do to cover that problem and to keep things moving efficiently."

Many trucks are equipped with on-board weighing systems that actually measure the weight of the load as the truck is filled. The driver gets a digital display and the shovel operator sees a set of lights—green, amber, and red. When the amber light shows, the truck will take one more bucket of material. These systems are quite accurate, to less than 5 percent. They avoid excessive weights because that over-stresses tires, drive motors, and the frame. And some materials are heavier per cubic yard than others; experience counts here. And when the shovel operator honks the horn, you're full and it is time to go.

"The 830s are so stable that you can't get one to slide," Debbie says. "They will lumber a bit, and if they are heavily loaded they might sink into the roadway a bit, if it is wet, but that's about all. The 830s are *wonderful, wonderful* trucks! They are absolutely marvelous, for being that big—they ride like a Cadillac. They are great trucks! We are *spoiled*."

When the rain or snow turns the road to mud and the wheels start to slip and slide, it only takes a call from one driver to get the whole fleet to pull to the side of the road while a load of gravel is imported to the slick spot for improved traction.

Chapter 3

WISEDA

Unless you are in the mining business you probably have never heard of the WISEDA company, but it is a small firm that is a big player in the market for really big trucks. It pioneered the 240-ton design back in 1982, and has offered a lot of innovations before and since.

The company was founded only in 1980 by William S. Davis who had previously been a part-owner of another off-highway truck manufacturer; he and his family still own it. Davis worked for other mine truck builders, thought he had a better way of doing things, and set up shop with some other veterans of the industry. He bought out the assets of a defunct truck builder and set out to build a bigger, better mousetrap, built on the experience of Davis

Opposite page, the four big discs that look like they might be headlights are actually air cleaner intakes on this WISEDA 2450. Dust is a significant problem in the mines, even though water trucks routinely sprinkle the roads to keep it under control.

and the veteran designers he recruited for the new company. Davis's company rapidly became a dominant force in the business.

Davis's interest in a new and larger design coincided with General Electric's development of the 787 drive motor and alternator system. One of the key players, WISEDA's current Vice President of Engineering, Bill Lewis, explains: "WISEDA believed that a larger hauler could be built that would provide the same economies of scale that we had when we moved from 85-ton to 100-ton, from 120 to 150, to 170, to 190-ton. The critical components were there: tires, engines, drive system—all were available. It turned out to be, as we thought, the next generation of truck size, that the economies of scale were there. The truck is now the 'bread-and-butter' size of the industry.

"The electric drive truck does a better job of 'loading' the engine, preventing some of the mechanical shock effects you get with a mechanical drive truck. We are

KING OF THE LODE

3482

Opposite page, the top of the bed extension reaches about 50ft from the ground during dumping of this WISEDA 2450. Dump angle is 50deg; it takes 24sec for the body to fully tilt up, powered by two three-stage hydraulic cylinders under 2400psi.

Above, ready to be serviced by the big Hitachi loader, this massive 2450 "King of the Lode" waits for half a million pounds of gold ore. WISEDA ships these trucks all over the world—in pieces.

seeing 18-20,000 hours of operation before overhaul; Caterpillar is looking at 10-12,000 hours before overhaul. The total operating costs in dollars-per-operating-hour are *quite* a bit lower with an electric drive than a mechanical drive truck."

According to WISEDA, component life expectancy for the mechanical-drive Cats is a lot shorter than the electric-drive tech-

nology; Caterpillar, on the other hand, has a different perspective.

WISEDA now builds its trucks in a facility at Baxter Springs, Kansas. Each is essentially a custom truck, based on a standard design, assembled to the specifications of the particular mine. While other manufacturers offer a wide range of designs and capacities, WISEDA specializes in the very

Above, you can't get much more material aboard. Even those big tires are showing the effect of the load. This WISEDA is jamming along at about 30mph.

Left, the ore is nicely pulverized by the application of explosives, making it easy for the shovel to scoop it up and deposit it aboard this WISEDA truck.

largest, 220- and 240-ton designs, and only sells diesel-electric-powered vehicles.

One of the major problems for trucks of this type is cracking of frame elements, a result of the tremendous stresses that are inflicted on the vehicle when 50 cubic yards of rock and dirt are dumped into the bed, or when the truck negotiates the twists and turns of a mine haul road. These stresses invariably destroy frames over time, and all builders adopt special steels and strong designs to cope. WISEDA's solution puts extra steel into the frame itself, about 25 percent more than some competing haul

trucks. For the KL-2450, that works out to about 12 percent of the total weight of the truck invested in the frame, compared to 9 percent in other large haul trucks.

WISEDA has a very strict quality control program that documents all the materials used, right down to details like who did the welding and how much welding rod or wire was used. Heat treatment of the frame is measured and documented, then inspected with ultrasonic devices to very strict standards. WISEDA can pull up this kind of history for any truck they've built. As a result, WISEDA warrants the frame for 60,000 operating hours or ten years, the longest in the industry.

Opposite page, in a view that's slightly distorted by a wide-angle lens, it's apparent that the right front tire is a long way from the driver's seat, and one of the things new drivers have a hard time with is judging where that tire is.

Above, tucked into the shovel, this tidy 2450's driver waits for the shovel operator to dump a load aboard. While he's waiting, you can get a peek at the steering gear and suspension.

Chapter 4

Caterpillar

The Caterpillar company has been the dominant force in construction equipment for many years and today sells a wide variety of mine trucks, loaders, scrapers, and hydraulic shovels.

Caterpillar and Dresser Company share the same hometown today, Peoria, Illinois, and were both born in the same, sleepy little California farm town many years ago. That town was Stockton, and the forerunners of the Caterpillar company set up shop here in the late 1800s. There were two companies at first, Holt Brothers and the Best Manufacturing Company; they merged in 1925 to form the Caterpillar Tractor Company. Holt already owned a plant in Peoria and after Caterpillar Tractor was formed and manufacture of construc-

The workhorse Cat 789 returns to the loader for yet another lap in the daily productivity race. Mechanical-drive trucks like this one are generally supposed to excel where mine road grades are moderate, and can be less efficient where the roads are steep.

tion equipment was consolidated there, where it remains—just up the street from another migrant from Stockton, the Komatsu Dresser Company.

While Dresser Company and Unit Rig WISEDA were developing the diesel-electric-drive technology, Cat experimented with electric drive trucks in the sixties and seventies but stuck with the tried-and-true mechanical drivetrain. It uses that technology on all its trucks today, including five models with capacities from 35-240 tons. One of Cat's selling points for these vehicles, and for mechanical drive in general, is that fuel economy is better than diesel-electric.

Cat builds just about all its own components, including engines. For the biggest Cat, the 793, the engine is an 1800hp four-stroke turbocharged V-16 diesel with a 6.7in bore and 7.5in stroke (4211ci displacement). The pistons are fabricated from an aluminum alloy; they use three rings and are oil-spray cooled.

Above, the tires on the smaller trucks last only about 5,000 miles, compared to 7,500 or more for the bigger rigs.

Right, this Cat 777 gives us a peek under its fender at the massive brackets that attach the suspension components to the frame.

Cat's frame design is much more box-like than those of other manufacturers, with huge rectangular beams and cross-members. The 789's frame uses two forgings and twenty castings for extra strength at the brackets for the front strut mount, rear suspension pivots, and the hoist cylinder pivot points.

Cat's globe-hopping senior salesman, Gene Holman, describes the line-up: "We make six models of truck, from 35- to 240-ton capacity. We introduced the 35-ton truck to the market in 1963, the 50-ton in 1970, six years later we introduced the 85-ton truck, then in 1985 the 150-ton truck, then in 1987 we co-introduced the 195, then in 1991 we started shipping the 240-ton truck. We used to be in construction

A clean, tidy, and apparently low-mileage Cat 789 awaits its turn for the attentions of the wheel loader. One of the virtues of these somewhat smaller trucks (small only when compared to the 240-ton rigs) is that they work with existing scoops, shovels, and loaders—unlike the big boys that require monster shovels to be at all efficient.

trucks for use on dams, then our 35- and 50-ton trucks started getting used on smaller eastern coal mines. Then, with the 85-ton, we started to move into some gold mines. When we brought out the 150 in 1985, that

Opposite page, that's about 12 cubic yards of gold ore pouring out of the Cat 992 wheel loader into the bed of this Cat 776/777 truck. If you could get at that gold—and you can't, because it is in microscopic particles—it would be worth approximately $100. In fact, this ore would have been considered virtually worthless during the Nevada gold rush years, and the costs of extracting the gold was more than the gold itself was worth until fairly recently. Even though gold prices are far lower than about ten years ago, mining efficiency is far higher—thanks in part to trucks like the Cat, along with the products of Dresser and WISEDA.

Opposite page top, the Cat 777 seems to be jamming right along but its rated cruise speed is no higher than trucks twice as big. That's about 30-35mph under the very best of conditions. But speed really is important; when coupled with safety, it represents higher production and bigger profits.

Opposite page bottom, this particular gold mine has used the Cat 777 tractor, normally supplied without dump body, and converted it to what is essentially a Cat model 777B. This truck is one of the smallest you'll find in the mines, with a gross vehicle weight of only 324,000lbs and a capacity of about 90 tons.

Above, despite the camouflage paint job, this isn't a Dresser in drag, but a mechanical-drive, 190-ton Caterpillar 789 truck, waiting its turn under the shovel. A wayward boulder seems to have scored a hit on the railing surrounding the cab. The body of the truck shows a lot of additional impacts, an unavoidable part of the program for mine haul trucks. Even so, the paint is fresh and neat; these trucks all get plenty of attention to the mechanical and cosmetic details.

was strictly a world class mine truck.

"The thing that makes us different from the other manufacturers is that we build essentially 100 percent of our trucks—the engine, the transmission, the drivetrain, the hydraulics—all of those are ours. Our competitors might make the frame and a couple of other major components, but they buy maybe 70 percent of each truck. These components are essentially out of their control. We at Cat control our components—that's a policy and a strategy.

"We are the world's only mechanical drive truck in the 150-, 190-, and 240-ton class. I've been around the electrical drive system since the sixties—and I think it is a pretty good system—but there are some inherent weaknesses to the system. The first one is that it has a single-speed transmission dictated by the final drive gear ratio. You are locked into a high- or a low-gear ratio. Cat trucks each come with six gear ratios; the driver can change the powertrain ratio. It boils down to what we call *powertrain efficiency.* All the engine horsepower rating tells you is how much fuel you can burn! The *only* horsepower rating that is important is the horsepower at the bottom of the tire on that rear axle.

"If you know the weight of the vehicle, the input horsepower, the grade, and the speed on that grade, you can calculate bottom-of-the-tire horsepower. You can calculate the efficiency of the truck by comparing the input hp with the tire hp—and for Caterpillar trucks, on a 0 to 15 percent grade, we'll put about 85 percent of that input power to the ground. Electric drive trucks will typically be about 72 percent. This means that we can move material at a lower fuel cost per ton of material moved."

Cat also makes some other interesting

claims. One is that an operator only really needs one kind of maintenance technician, mechanics. Electric-drive trucks need mechanics *and* electronic technicians. "We tend to run on fewer hours of maintenance than electric-drive," Holman says. "There are about 8,500 hours in a year, and we have Cat trucks that consistently run 7,000-7,400 hours a year; that is *very* difficult to do with electric-drive trucks."

Cat uses oil-cooled disc brakes on all four corners. Other builders use disc brakes in combination with retarders. Even so, Cat's Gene Holman claims its braking system absorbs horsepower with the efficiency of a Formula 1 race car. "We can de-accelerate an 830,000lb vehicle from 30mph in *seventy five feet*! You can't do that with an electric-drive truck; they take from 120-150ft under the same conditions.

"In a way," Gene says, "the cycle times for these trucks are similar to lap times for a race car; your cycle or lap times are somewhat dependent on how comfortable that driver is about 'hanging it out.' Some of these mine haul drivers have been doing this for twenty or twenty-five years. They are incredibly sensitive to the vehicle and the way it behaves on a mine road. If they feel safe, they are going to perform at a higher level than if they are not."

Chapter 5

Dresser Company

Dresser Company's ancestry in the construction trades goes back to 1922 and a land-leveling project near Stockton, California. That's when a gent named R. G. LeTourneau developed a new, improved version of the scraper. Scrapers have been around for centuries, both horse- and man-powered, and by 1922 the basic design had been adapted by many manufacturers for use with trucks and tractors. LeTourneau's version was stronger, based on a welded frame, and was much more efficient than previous models. He formed a company to sell the design, the R. G. LeTourneau Company.

LeTourneau motorized the scraper the

Opposite page, the size of truck that will work best in a particular mine will depend on many factors; bigger is not always better, and sometimes the biggest trucks are just too big. This one has a capacity of 200 tons, or about 80 percent of the largest currently available. Even so, this Dresser Haulpak 685E tips the scales at about 250,000lb empty; it stands 21ft high and is almost 24ft across. *Komatsu Dresser/Haulpak*

next year, another innovation. Stockton must have been the approximate center of the construction equipment industry about that time, because Caterpillar was also started in the same little agricultural town (although much earlier), and there must have been quite a bit of cross-fertilization among the engineers and mechanics working in the plants. Both companies departed Stockton for Peoria, Illinois, so their descendants still work in the same community—perhaps accounting for the lively and innovative tradition of competition between the two firms that continues today.

The R. G. LeTourneau Company was absorbed into the Westinghouse Air Brake Company, (WABCO), and the Haulpak truck division was sold to Dresser Company Construction and Mining Equipment Company in 1984. Dresser Company and the Japanese firm of Komatsu Ltd. set up a joint-venture in 1988, the current company called Komatsu Dresser Company—the

Above, here comes Kerr-McGee's No. 2030, a Dresser 630E with the Hi-Vol aftermarket bed. Just think, if somebody would just build a cab-over camper for these things, you could have a "land yacht" that could include its own garden.

Left, here comes another 50 tons of overburden into the bed of this Dresser 630E. When the scoop unloads, the whole truck wallows under the impact of 50 tons or so, dropping into the back.

world's second-largest builder of heavy construction equipment.

The important name to remember in all this is *Haulpak*—a name that goes back to the first pioneer of the breed, way back in 1957. That's when WABCO introduced the very first rough, tough, high-capacity construction and mining truck. It was a 32-ton-capacity model—immense for its time—with mechanical drive. That truck revolutionized the business of moving large vol-

Above, here's another view of the Phillipi-Hagenbuch "Hi-Vol" custom body, in this case on a Dresser 630E. Higher bed walls plus a tailgate allow more coal to be carried.

umes of dirt, rock, and ore, made the whole business far more economical that before.

The first diesel-electric drive truck wore a "Haulpak" label, too. That truck rolled out of the factory in 1964. It didn't eliminate the mechanical-drive technology from the industry—Haulpak still sells three models of that type—but it made possible the much larger vehicles that have developed over the intervening thirty years. Over 17,000 Haulpaks have been sold. The Komatsu Dresser Company claims that

there are more 100-ton and above Haulpaks in the mines than any competing make (mechanical or electric), and that Haulpaks have the lowest cost-per-ton for ownership and operation in the off-highway rear-dump truck market.

Regardless of the corporate name, the Haulpak division has made some important innovations over the years. Besides that first 32-ton truck and its diesel-electric drive descendant, Haulpak claims parentage to the two-axle, compact, tight-turning design for these big trucks. They also introduced the idea of using exhaust to heat the frame and the dump body to reduce cracking in cold weather; the deep-V shape to

Cost Per Hour (prorated)	830E Haulpak	793 Cat	MT4000 Unit Rig
Preventive maintenance	$1.97	$3.36	$2.17
Engine overhaul	$6.24	$6.61	$6.46
Engine-Programmed Maintenance	$1.20	$1.59	$1.24
Drive System Maintenance & Overhaul	$5.13	$10.35	$5.13
Spindles, Suspensions, Hydraulic Cylinders	$2.21	$2.33	$5.45
Brake System	$1.84	$2.58	$2.10
Other Repairs	$8.78	$9.25	$11.74
Tire Maintenance	$25.92	$25.22	$25.40
Dump Body Maintenance.	$1.67	$1.83	$2.01
Fuel & Lube	$41.82	$35.81	$40.45
Driver	$22.50	$22.50	$22.50
Total Operating Cost Per Hour	$119.28	$121.43	$124.65
Production Per Hour	756.1 tons	719.8 tons	706.9 tons

lower center-of-gravity; the big, round, extremely strong "horse-collar" frame; a specialized nitrogen-over-oil suspension system; and more recently a computer-driven Haulpack Management System (HMS).

The current line-up of Haulpak trucks range from the (comparatively) puny 140M, a 40-ton mechanical drive truck, to the 830E 240-ton diesel-electric. There are three mechanical-drive models and five electrics.

The Codelco Company operates one of the world's largest mining truck fleets at its Chuquicamata, Chile, mine. Based on actual productivity measurements at the mine, and using typical US operating costs, the company did an operating cost comparison on the 830E, Cat's 793B, and the MT4000, all 240-ton mining trucks, in May of 1993, with representatives from each company observing and verifying the tests. The results, which are shown here, were a bit surprising.

The Cat 793B is a mechanical-drive truck while the other two use diesel-electric

There is plenty of room around the shovel, and on most haul roads, for maneuvering. You drive trucks like this Dresser 830E British-style, though, on the left. Although the roads are dirt, they are smooth and free of rocks—kept that way by a fleet of "blades" that constantly scurry around, keeping the streets clean. That's because a single rock falling off a truck can destroy a brand new $11,000 tire on a following vehicle if the driver doesn't see, or can't avoid, hitting it.

drive. The Cat had about an 8 percent fuel economy advantage as a result, but when the other cost elements were all calculated,

Above, the 630E and the bigger 830E can sometimes be difficult to tell apart, but one helpful breed characteristic is the front wheel hubs—they are a smooth, sheet metal cover on the smaller 630 truck, a ribbed casting on the larger 830.

those saving were offset by higher costs elsewhere. These results were based on a fairly short test period and might not be an accurate predictor of long-term, real world costs, but the test was at least based on vehicles with identical specifications, all operated in the same mine, on the same roads, hauling the same material. The mine is conducting a long-term test, the results of which aren't available at this writing.

This side view of the biggest Dresser shows the exhaust ports at the rear of the bed, part of the same type of system used by most mine haul truck builders to prevent cold-stress cracking during extreme weather conditions. You also get an idea of how the truck's designers built in protection for the cab compartment and the fore end of the truck from flying, falling objects like boulders—an occupational hazard for these vehicles.

Mega Dump Trucks—the Sequel

When the first big mine haul truck was built, thirty years ago, bystanders probably said (the way bystanders always do) that the 35-ton truck was the final word in truck development and that *nothing* bigger would or could possibly ever come down the road. The bystanders have been saying the same thing about the 240-ton truck, too, and they'll tell you that the tires are at their practical upper limit, that nothing bigger can be shipped by truck or train. That conventional wisdom, once again, seems to be wrong.

As Bill Lewis at WISEDA reports, "There are tire manufacturers looking at making tires two sizes larger than presently available, and—depending on the market—we are fifteen to twenty-two months from having larger tires on a larger truck. We believe that will be in the 300- to 350-ton capacity. It will be a six-tire, two axle truck, like the one we have today. The engine is already available from MTU, and Cummins is looking at building one, too. Tires are about two years away. Drivetrain manufacturers are starting to take an active interest. The market interest is there; a number of mine owners have expressed interest in 300-plus ton trucks.

"As today's mine operators become more experienced with these vehicles, and look at not just the direct acquisition cost but what the vehicle will cost over 60,000 hours, the electric-drive truck is the hands-down winner over the mechanical because of parts and maintenance costs."

BULLDOZERS

Sam Sargent and Michael Alves

Acknowledgments

The authors wish to thank everyone who contributed to this book, especially: Lee Woodward, Deere & Company; Joycelyn Luster and Marsha Hausser, Caterpillar, Inc.; John Giesfeldt, Nelson & Schmidt / Komatsu Dresser Company; Don Frantz and Eric Orlemann, Historical Construction Equipment Association; James Murray, Kiewit Pacific Company; Bill Larkin and Jerry Allen, Granite Rock; Lyle Miller and Dee Crawford, Rasmusson, Inc.; Sergio Gonzales, Sonoma County Public Works; Steve Stromgren, Operating Engineers Local 3; Captain Frank Childress, US Army, Ft. Irwin NTC; Stan Ghisletta and John Schlesiger, Peterson Equipment Company; George Beltrametti, Stony Point Rock Quarry, Inc.; and Rod Pedersen, California Division of Forestry; and Baron Wolman.

Preface

Every little boy has a fascination with heavy equipment. Some of us never outgrew it. In researching and photographing *Bulldozers*, we had the opportunity to experience firsthand the power of these heavy metal workhorses up close. For some people, climbing onto the track treads and swinging up into the cab of a dozer as the sun breaks the horizon is just the start of another day. For us, it was the experience of a lifetime. Driving a dozer is definitely a power trip.

We traveled to America's heartland to see how dozers rise from molten metal, visiting such cities as Peoria, Illinois, headquarters of Caterpillar, Inc., and Dubuque, Iowa, where John Deere dozers are built. We shot dozers at dawn and dusk and in the dark all over the country. Whenever we drove the freeways, we kept a sharp eye out for dozers at work. A business trip to Hawaii even yielded unexpected but welcome shots of yellow bulldozers working the red earth of cane fields in Kauai. What we found was that wherever there's dirt, there are dozers.

We tried to show a broad range of dozers and how they're used in the field. In this book, you'll see the dozers we saw at work, rest, and retirement. It's a close-up look at some very big blades.

Who Took the "Bull" Out of Bulldozers?

How did "a dose fit for a bull" become "a track-type tractor fitted with a broad steel blade in front, used for removing obstacles and leveling uneven surfaces"?

Well, around 1880, the common usage of "bull-dose" in the United States meant administering a large and efficient dose of any sort of medicine or punishment. If you "bull-dosed" someone, you gave him a severe whipping or coerced or intimidated him in some other way, such as by holding a gun to his head. This must have happened pretty often, because by 1886, with a slight variation in spelling, a "bulldozer" had come to mean both a large-caliber pistol and the person who wielded it. In short, these were people and weapons that got things done in an efficient, if somewhat blunt, manner. Anything that got in their way was leveled. So, naturally, by the late 1800s, "bulldozing" came to mean using brawny force to push over, or through, any obstacle.

It wasn't really until 1930, after the introduction of the "crawler" or "track-type" tractor, that the term bulldozing also came to be commonly associated with the act of earth moving, specifically by using a large, slightly curved, steel blade attached to the front of a tractor to push things around.

And if you want to be technically correct, a "bulldozer" actually only refers to the blade of a track-type tractor, not the combination of the two, but this distinction has blurred with time and usage. It seems the frequent pairing of a front-mounted steel blade on a track-type tractor led to the whole assembly commonly being called a bulldozer.

Actually, no one in the bulldozer business even calls their equipment a bulldozer anymore. They're just called "dozers" by the people who use them, and when they're working, they're "dozing"—which could never be confused with someone taking a light rest or nap.

Chapter 1

A Little History

Left
Diesel engines fueled the birth of more powerful bulldozers such as this mid-thirties Caterpillar Diesel Seventy-Five pulling a three-shank ripper. The "D" in Caterpillar's famous D-series track-type tractors comes from Cat's first diesel V-8. The D17000 engine powered the RD8 tractor, later known just as the dependable Cat D8. *Caterpillar, Inc.*

Above
Following the First World War, the Best Company—which in 1925 merged with the Holt Manufacturing Company to form Caterpillar Tractor Company—introduced a new machine. The year was 1921, and the machine was the advanced-for-its-time, gas-powered, enclosed-cab Best 30 "Tracklayer." It's shown here fitted with a light-duty dozer blade. Constant improvements of these track-type tractors— also called crawlers—by Caterpillar and other manufacturers provided the power and performance needed. *Caterpillar, Inc.*

War means work even in the worst weather.
Removing rubble in bomb-damaged Great Britain
required the services of many lend-lease
shipments, including this Caterpillar D7.
Caterpillar, Inc.

Water Tanks for Mesopotamia

There's an interesting story in the evolution of the crawler tractor—the power behind the bulldozer blade—from hard-working farm vehicle to gun-toting tank.

In September of 1914, engineers from the Holt Manufacturing Company were dispatched to England to demonstrate the capability of Holt's "Caterpillar" crawler tractors to haul artillery and supplies under World War I battlefield conditions. In turn, the British War Department sent an officer to Holt's East Peoria, Illinois, plant to learn what he could about these powerful American machines.

Earlier, Ernest Swinton, a British lieutenant colonel (soon to be credited as the father of the modern tank) had developed the idea of an armored "machine gun destroyer" to help break the deadly stalemate of trench warfare. Upon hearing from military friends of an American farm tractor that could "climb like hell," Swinton convinced British manufacturers to add machine guns and cannons to a radically new type of armored crawler tractor. Prototypes of the new machines were dubbed "Water Tanks for Mesopotamia" both to conceal their military mission and because the new enclosed equipment did bear some resemblance to a tubby water tank.

Used experimentally for the first time in the Battle of the Somme in September 1916, the new tanks were only mildly successful; however, seeing their bullets bounce off the tanks had serious demoralizing effects on the entrenched German troops. Slowly gaining tactical experience, the British eventually were able to use the tank's ability to punch across trench lines decisively in the Battle of Cambrai—forever changing the combatants' bloody trench tactics and even shortening the war, according to some experts. The German army also manufactured a few tanks, but estimates are that throughout the war they were able to put only about twenty into action, with little result.

Although no American-built tractors were employed as armed tanks during World War I, more than 10,000 Caterpillar crawlers saw service on the Allies' side as weapons and equipment carriers. By the end of the war, the peaceful powerhouse called a crawler tractor had found a new role as warrior. In 1918, Swinton himself even visited the Holt factory to pay tribute to what he called " the cradle of the tank."

The "Boss of the Beach" was often an armored tractor driven by a combat engineer. Track-type tractors fitted with bulldozer blades were used on every front in World War II to clear mines, build landing strips, and, in more than one instance, charge an enemy-held position under withering fire. One war correspondent tells the story of a small convoy of crawlers that were badly needed to build a road in a valley far below the mountaintop where they were located. To get them down so that they could build the road, engineers simply rolled the driverless dozers off the edge of the cliff, letting them tumble down the mountainside. According to the correspondent, not one machine was put out of action. If they didn't land on their tracks, the soldiers just pushed them upright. All were driven immediately into duty. *Caterpillar, Inc.*

For more than twenty years, Caterpillar's powerful D9—introduced in 1954—was the company's largest dozer. Its bulldozer blade was raised and lowered by using a cable-and-pulley assembly. *Caterpillar, Inc.*

John Deere dozers carved a construction niche during the boom years of the fifties and sixties. Bulldozers changed the face of America by helping to build millions of miles of roads and leveling the land for every American's dream— a house. *Deere & Company*

Chapter 2

Bulldozer Builders

Left
Among them—Dave Rinker, Carl Ballard, Fred Vaughn, and Terry Bode—have more than 113 years of experience building bulldozers for John Deere.

Above
To ensure complete coverage, various parts of the bulldozer are painted separately. A dozer's coiled tracks are shown here as they emerge dripping wet from a paint bath.

The heart of every bulldozer is the engine. Here, Robert Pluemer readies a 550 series engine for mating to a dozer on John Deere's utility crawler tractor assembly line. John Deere's larger dozers are also assembled in the 1.2 mile-long Dubuque, Iowa, manufacturing facility, which has five million square feet of manufacturing space under one roof.

Les Simmons and Benny Martensen lower a large B-series dozer onto its tracks. The massive U-frame assembly is the attachment point for the bulldozer's blade. At John Deere's Dubuque Works, as soon as the crawlers are fully tracked, they are driven to the next assembly area within the 1.2 mile-long plant. In a field operation, putting the tracks on a bulldozer would take at least 30 minutes. On the assembly line, it takes less than 10 minutes.

An 8-ton, G-series bulldozer rides an overhead track on its way to the painting booth. John Deere's standard construction equipment color is yellow, but the company will custom paint any color a customer orders.

A large John Deere 750B crawler is prepped in the painting booth by technician Charlie Leppert. It takes about 6 gallons (gal) of lead-free, "JDMF9LA-Industrial Yellow" to paint the company's smaller G-series dozer.

If One's Good, Two Are Better

If your biggest tractor isn't big enough, what do you do? Well, you might try putting two together. In 1969, that's just what the Caterpillar Tractor Company did with the introduction of the side-by-side SxSD9G and the Quad-Track DD9G. Each of these unique models featured two connected D9G track-type tractors working in sync: The SxS used two tractors coupled together to push a single bulldozer blade; while the Quad-Track put two tractors in tandem—nose to tail—to provide more power to shove a scraper.

Manufactured from 1974-1977, the 92-ton SxSD9H version used two Model D353 six-cylinder, four-stroke diesel engines—each with a displacement of 1,473ci—to develop a total of 820hp. The two tractors were connected at three points: at the rear with a 16in-diameter structural-steel tubular tie bar; in the center with a box-construction brace between the track frames; and at the front by the 7ft, 2in high, 24ft long bulldozer blade. The whole machine was operated by one person from the left tractor. In a turn, power was supplied to three of the four tracks. The two units could also be separated and run individually if needed.
Photo copyright by Eric Orlemann

Harnessing the power of two D9H tractors was the 770hp DD9G (which was replaced in 1974 by the DD9H). Although the entire Quad-Track arrangement was discontinued by Caterpillar after 1980, several examples are still working in the US. Dual controls allow the joined unit to be operated by one person from either machine, or the pair can

be disconnected and used as two single tractors. Only the lead tractor came fitted with a bulldozer blade; a blade and hydraulic control were available as optional equipment for the rear tractor. The approximate shipping weight for the DD9G was 175,000lb, about 87.5 tons. *Photo copyright by Eric Orlemann*

An impressive line of John Deere dozers awaits shipment from Iowa to the far corners of the earth. Even the worldwide International Standards Organization (ISO) is impressed by the quality of John Deere's machines. The company's Dubuque Works is one of only two US equipment manufacturers to have met the prestigious ISO 9001 standard for quality.

Bound for Russia's Yamal Peninsula in the Arctic Circle, these Peoria, Illinois-built Caterpillar D9Ns are part of a 295-tractor deal with Russia's largest natural gas corporation, GAZPROM. The $100 million sale was part of President Clinton's promised $1.6 billion aid package to the Commonwealth of Independent States. *Caterpillar, Inc.*

Chapter 3

School of Hard Rocks

In the small town of Rancho Murieta, California, Local 3 of the Union of Operating Engineers runs an annual apprenticeship training program for students from forty-six northern California counties. Annually, the 23-year-old program teaches approximately 150 people the fine art and subtle skills of operating heavy equipment. No experience is necessary. A written application is all that it takes to apply. Housed and fed by the union for the first five weeks of the program, hopeful dozer apprentices start out by learning the basics of earth moving—grade setting, cutting, and filling. By the time they receive a certificate of completion, they've spent more than 6,400hr of operating time in the driver's seat. Although wages vary by location, experience, and company, northern California bulldozer operators average about $24 per hour. With benefits, the total compensation package adds up to about $45 per hour. Steady work depends on the economy.

Left
With his dozer's back-up beeper blaring, David Floyd of Cotati, California, rips neatly through the edge of a bluff during a day of training on a D6D. He's a "Stage 4" operator, with nearly enough hours to earn his certificate.

Driving a Dozer Isn't What It Seems

At first glance, you'd think driving a dozer was easy. It's not. But if you ask just about anybody who runs one for a living, their first dozer experience came when they were still in their tender teens. It seems age 12 is the perfect time to begin driving dozers—oops, *operating* dozers; "Teamsters *drive*, operating engineers *operate*," according to dozer instructor Deane Sweet, the man who put me at the controls of a Caterpillar D4H.

Most people who make a career out of operating heavy equipment started by growing up using large pieces of machinery like dozers "down on the farm" early in their lives. They're comfortable making machines respond to their commands—commands like go, stop, turn, don't run over that. It's basic stuff, but there's hardly anybody who's a smooth dozer operator right off the bat. This is a skill that takes time to develop.

The first thing is, you don't just put the blade down and go. That's not to say you can't, but if you have the ambition to cut a nice, level road without camel-sized humps, it would help to develop the eye-hand-foot coordination of Joe Montana before you try to do it with a dozer.

Dozers are big, and you can't actually see what you're pushing with that blade out front. You've got to "feel" the steel respond to pressure, watch how much dirt is spilling off the side of the blade, and constantly make small adjustments. Generally, the blade controls are to your right, and the track controls are to your left. You decelerate the dozer's engine by pushing the throttle lever down with your right foot. If it operated like a car (down for fast), you couldn't hold the pedal down after a long day of bouncing around in a dozer cab. You brake with your left foot.

The D4H I used was equipped with a "six-way" blade, that is, you could position it up or down, tilt it left or right, or angle it either direction using a single lever on the right of the driver's seat. The track controls use two levers, one for each track. If you pull up on the left lever just a little, the left track slows and you begin slowly turning left. If you pull the lever farther back, the track locks and you make a very hard left-hand swing. (You can almost turn a dozer in its own length this way.) To move, you just take your foot off the decelerator and switch between the two track levers, depending on which way you want to go and how fast you want to turn. Shifting into reverse requires throwing a third lever.

After giving me a brief explanation of the controls and showing me how to use the two-way radio all dozer trainees wear to get instructions—and warning me that the rollover protection system was good for only one roll—Sweet retreated to the safety of his van as I fired up my D4 and headed out for my first try at pushing a little dirt around the union's training site at Rancho Murieta.

Actually, I wasn't bad; Sweet says he's seen worse. (Nice of him to say that.)

I swung the high-tracked D4H around a big old D8H and proceeded to make a nice, straight pass with the blade cutting turned-up soil about a foot deep. So much for beginner's luck.

On my next pass, I tried to dig a little deeper. Then it happened. I got behind the machine. As I lowered the blade, the dozer pitched down and slowed down. To compensate, I raised the blade. That got me back to speed, but now my blade was too high. So I lowered it. It dug in. I slowed down. So I raised it... well, you can guess the rest.

As I looked back at the roller coaster road I'd just created, I vowed never to waste my money renting a bulldozer I planned to use myself. It's a power trip, but if I need something done with a dozer, I'll leave operating it to an operating engineer.

Fifty-eight-year-old Deane Sweet has been teaching the techniques of bulldozer operation at Rancho Murieta for the past seven years. He started running dozers when he was 12. At one point in his career, to finish a job, he ran a dozer twenty-four straight hours without taking a break. Dozer instructors and students are linked by radio so that the secrets of such smooth operators as Deane Sweet can be passed on more efficiently. Experienced instructors can tell right away if someone has potential; a few who don't have the necessary eye-hand-foot coordination, depth perception, and patience to learn the trade get washed out every year.

Formerly the site of an old placer gold mine, the union's 80-acre training area is now part of a sprawling ranch. Large cuts in the gently rolling hills were carved by miners using water cannons during the 1800s. In a mutually beneficial deal, the rancher who owns the land lets the union's dozer operators train there in return for restoring the site to a more natural configuration.

Lisa Honeein has what it takes to make a fine dozer operator, according to Deane Sweet, her instructor. The Santa Cruz resident grew up operating farm equipment.

One of about 160 female operating engineers in California, Lisa Honeein regularly works out with a 14-ton Caterpillar D6C at the union's school.

The beginning of another long day at dozer
school is just the start of this operating engineer's
career. The union offers training in a wide variety
of heavy equipment.

Chapter 4

Big Deals

Left
Paul Smith flew out to Turlock, California from Wauconda, Illinois, to test drive this used Caterpillar D5H LGP for his brother's excavating firm. With about 1,500 operating hours on the engine—which Smith considers about a year's worth of work in Illinois—this dozer is on the market for $77,000. Brand new, it cost around $150,000. Publications such as *Rock & Dirt,* published in Crossville, Tennessee, help buyers and sellers of heavy equipment find each other.

Above
The wider-track shoes and longer undercarriage help this Caterpillar dozer work especially well in soft ground. The distinctive tracks are self-cleaning Apex mud pads that don't pick up as much muck. Smith put the dozer through its paces by digging a 5ft hole in United Equipment's test track and filling it back in, working the Cat crawler into tight angles and moving loads of dirt to shake out any potential problems in the used machine. After a 30min test drive, he was ready to deal.

Redwood tread substitutes for steel track on this one-of-a-kind, "walk-in" bulldozer. The building's architect, Cliff Cheney, included steel shift levers on the roof of the two-story bulldozer to lend even more authenticity to the design. It's got to be the only dozer with a permanent street address.

You can't miss United Equipment's building along busy Highway 99 in the small town of Turlock, California. Built in 1976 by the company's owner, Harold Logsdon, the 21ft-high, 28ft-wide, 66ft-long, realistic looking bulldozer is made from redwood and plywood. Complete with steel and aluminum hydraulics, it houses the firm's sales offices. That's a 7ft-tall Cat D4D parked in front of the building. If this wooden bulldozer had an engine, it could push a load much bigger than the 6ft-high mound of sand and rocks piled in front.

This old D8H uses a cable-and-pulley assembly
to raise and lower the blade. Like wrinkled skin,
the well-worn blade testifies to long years of hard
work in the sun. Today, a comparable, fresh-from-
the-factory D8H would cost about $350,000.

Dozers: Facts and Figures

How Many Bulldozers are There in the US?

Equipment Data Associates estimates that at any one time, there are about 116,000 operating dozers in America. Forty-three percent of this fleet—that's about 50,000 bulldozers—were purchased new between 1987 and 1992.

Building, highway, and heavy construction firms own approximately 60 percent of all operating bulldozers in the US, but mining and materials firms bought 30 percent of all new dozers.

How Long Do Dozers Last?

According to a survey by *Construction Equipment* magazine, this is how it breaks out.

Average hours at retirement for different size dozers:

Under 100hp	12,000
100 to 200hp	16,500
More than 200hp	19,500

It's obvious that bigger dozers live longer.

Average annual operating hours for different dozer owners:

Building Contractors	1,130
Highway/heavy Contractors	1,290
General Heavy Contractors	1,430
Materials Producers	2,500
Utilities	1,040
Mining	2,760
Government	740
Other Non-Construction	1,250

Perhaps the President might put those low-hour government dozers to work in Washington, D.C. Getting a bill pushed through Congress could definitely be done a lot quicker from the seat of a bulldozer.

How Much Does a Dozer Cost?

According to estimates compiled by Equipment Data Associates, expect to pay around $78,000 for a new 100hp machine. If you want something in the 500hp range, you'll pay about $370,000. A new D11N will set you back nearly $900,000.

Most people buy this type of equipment. In 1991, only 9 percent of dozer users rented; however, that's triple the number of renters there were in 1987, according to one study.

What's the world's biggest dozer?

The Komatsu 575A-2 earns that honor. It has a 1050hp engine and tips the scales at 291,010lb.

What's the largest American-made dozer?

Caterpillar's D11N weighs 214,847 lb and rolls along courtesy of a 770hp V-8 engine. It's built in Peoria, Illinois.

Chapter 5

Fire Fighter

Left
Former F-14 Navy Fighter Pilot Gary Beverlin dons a fireproof, cloth-lined, communications-equipped racing helmet modified with a filtered air breathing system for close-in fire fighting with his Fiat-Allis HD-11EP dozer. In this machine, Beverlin, a California Division of Forestry (CDF) heavy fire equipment operator, can work smoke-shrouded hills with grades as steep as 70 percent. The formerly stock tractor received a CARCO F-50 winch, full ROPS (Roll-Over Protection Structure), brush screens, dust filter, belly guards, an extra set of side-mounted lights, and several other modifications by the CDF before it qualified as a fire fighter. It sports a 12ft, 6in-long manual angle and tilt blade.

Above
Since Beverlin's dozer is part of an "initial response unit," rolling to every CDF fire call in the dry hills north of Healdsburg, California, speed is important. Beverlin routinely has the 43,000-lb HD-11EP unchained, fired up, and off the Fruehauf Tilt-Top trailer within 3-5min of arriving at a blaze. The trailer actually performs a balancing act. Unlocked but not unhitched, it splits in the middle as the weight of the tractor shifts, allowing the dozer to back directly onto the ground. To avoid "wide-load" road requirements while en route to the fire, the dozer's blade is set at a 45 degree angle to minimize its width. The entire setup is towed by the CDF's 1980 GMC Brigadier dual-axle truck.

The upside-down license plate is an "in" joke among CDF dozer crews. Another dozer driver had a similar upside-down plate, one he mounted inside a license plate holder with the inscription "If you can read this, turn me over." Fortunately,

Beverlin has never rolled his dozer while on the job, but his HD-11EP's ROPS is certified for up to three rolls before requiring reinspection. Notice the two canteens and extra set of backup lights above the winch.

The CDF protects its dozer operators in a variety of ways. Beverlin's HD-11EP is outfitted with roll-down, reflective aluminum fire curtains on three sides of the cab. He breathes filtered—but not cooled—air through his helmet. The air is scrubbed of smoke and pesticide residue by charcoal filters inside the 3M-built agricultural air filtration unit shown behind his right shoulder. The helmet is also fitted with a communications microphone and earphones. In the upper right of the cab is an eighty-channel Midland radio that Beverlin uses to stay in touch with various other firefighters, including those flying air tankers. If the dozer is about to be overrun by swiftly moving flames, the operator can signal for an air drop of fire retardant on his bulldozer in one of two ways. He can either call in a tanker on the radio, or by turning on the aircraft strobe beacon light mounted in the roof of the dozer's cab. If that fails, the only things left are the cab's heat shields, a portable fire extinguisher, a protective fire blanket, and the burn kit that every dozer driver carries.

Immediately after the liberation of Kuwait during the 1991 Gulf War, Caterpillar D8Ns and D9Ns were used to help put out hundreds of oil well fires. *Caterpillar, Inc.*

Chapter 6

Road Builder

Left
Near Cloverdale, California, a Cat D9L with a single-shank ripper starts a day's work on a freeway bypass around the city. C. A. Rasmusson contractors blasted a mountain of rock for the Highway 101 bypass, then used dozers to move it.

Above
Two of Kiewit Pacific Construction's Caterpillar D10 dozers team up to push a scraper leveling a roadbed under construction near Hayward, California.

A Kiewit Pacific CAT D9N dozer rips the bed for a new super-highway in California. Mounted on the rear of the tractor is a hydraulically operated, twin-shank parallelogram ripper that can cut nearly 32in deep, with a penetration force of nearly 33,000lb. Once the dirt is loosened, a scraper can scoop it up and transport it. Notice the Cat tractor's unique elevated sprocket undercarriage. According to Caterpillar, this design helps to increase traction and reduce maintenance.

Working with almost choreographed precision, four Caterpillar crawlers move in a veritable bulldozer ballet. Two dozers push a scraper as it piles up a load of soil, while two others rip the ground, loosening the dirt for the next scraper pass. Millions of tons of earth are moved from the construction site this way.

A protruding hard point on the rear of the scraper, called a "stinger," is what the dozer's blade pushes against. It's usually slathered in grease to protect against metal-on-metal wear.

Neither rock nor dirt stands in the way of a determined dozer driver. This D9L operator pushes a massive load down what is to become a California freeway.

239

Rectangular steel "wear plates" are welded to the sides of this dozer's Beales-manufactured blade. Abrasive materials such as rock then wear out the wear plates—which can be easily replaced— instead of the blade.

Sporting a huge "slope board" like an outstretched arm, a Cat D9L outfitted with a single-shank ripper heads for the hills. Various-sized slope boards are used for grading angles on hills. They're mounted on the side of the dozer, and raised or lowered hydraulically so that the bulldozer can cut a slope or terrace without making a steep traverse across the hill.

This Cat D10N is using a short, side-mounted grading blade to cut an angle. With various attachments, the bulldozer becomes a versatile earthmover that can shape the landscape to exacting specifications.

Next page
Bulldozer work is often needed even after a road is built. To keep from tearing up the road, this CASE-built 550E uses a steel-corded rubber track instead of a traditional metal track. *J. I. Case Company*

A Cat D3 dozer driver adjusts the angle of a spade nose blade used for cutting small trenches. It's unique attachments like these that let bulky bulldozers move and reshape the ground exactly as planners and developers desire.

A single pass with a spade nose blade quickly cuts a neat furrow between the little D3's tracks.

Caterpillar's most massive dozer is the D11N. It's 14ft, 11in tall, 12ft wide, and sports a 37,239lb, 8ft-high, 20ft-long U-blade with a capacity of 45 yards of material. It weighs in at 214, 847lb with full fuel and a single-shank ripper. A four-stroke, 770hp V-8 engine with a 388gal diesel fuel tank keeps the D11N going. Optional equipment includes both a 161lb air conditioner and a 450lb "Arctic package." Base price is a little more than $890,000. *Photo copyright by Eric Orlemann*

Chapter 7

Rock Crusher

Who Are These Guys?

It seems as if every bulldozer operator we met while researching this book was cut from similar cloth. As a group, they were straight-talking, no-nonsense, firm-hand-shake, likeable guys who started driving dozers down on the farm. And generally, they exuded energy.

We met guys like 69-year-old Buck Piazza of Penngrove, California, who leaped down from his dozer's 10ft-high cab in one step when we asked to take his picture. "Anything I can do. Where do you want it?" said Piazza, helpfully. When we asked him to run the dozer up the side of a huge boulder and pound away at the seemingly solid rock, he obliged without a moment's hesitation, churning his huge D9L up a slippery slope to plow away pieces for a photo.

In other chapters of this book, you'll read

A Komatsu bulldozer cuts a quarry terrace. Pushing a mass of rock and dirt before it, the dozer cuts into the hill to create a shelf from which to work. Somebody's got to be the first one to carve his way up or down a slope, and no one's better equipped than a man with a bulldozer.

about guys like Mike Pieper, an Iowa farmer we met as he worked round-the-clock to build a pumping station to drain 14,000 acres of flooded farmland. Unable to drive our car along the soggy levee to the construction site, we hitched a ride on Pieper's Honda all-terrain vehicle—the three of us barreling along the top of the dike on a bike built for one. To get back to the road after taking pictures, Pieper's cousin Carl fired up a small skiff and boated us over the family farm, ruined by a 48hr flood of Mississippi River mud and water. It was the kind of devastation that would crush lesser men. But to men like Pieper, it was just another obstacle to overcome, a job that needed to be done—and that's what a dozer does best.

As one British officer in World War II said after meeting bulldozer operators, "Most of them are damned fools about their machines. They have utterly no fear, drive the things everywhere nonchalantly, and get mad as the devil if shells or bullets hit their beloved machines...they all chew tobacco, swear magnificently, never bathe, and are so very adept at repair that it is a matter of pride with them not to ask repair crews for help."

With the early morning sun rising behind him, 69-year-old Buck Piazza of Penngrove, California, fires up his Caterpillar D9L for another day of making big rocks into little ones. Rock crushing operations are wonderful examples of what happens when an immovable object meets an irresistible force—like a 100,000lb Cat crawler. With his Cat tractor's massive ripper poised like some deadly giant claw, Piazza attacks his quarry head on...

Buck gets a blade full...

To all the dozer operators who posed for our pictures, thank you. You bring to mind a famous phrase uttered in a movie about Butch Cassidy and the Sundance Kid. In scene after scene, Butch and Sundance are relentlessly pursued by Pinkerton agents bent on their arrest. No matter what they do, Butch and Sundance can't shake the agents. Each time Butch looks back at the tireless, rugged riders bearing down on them, he says "Who *are* those guys?" They're guys who didn't give up, didn't give in, and just did their job…just like you.

…gives a little shove…and turns another rock into a rock pile. Of course, his "little shove" could probably level a house.

A large part of the quarry business is separating the good rocks from the bad. Here, a dozer operator slices a path between mounds of sorted rock.

Dick Carber works for Wendling Quarries, Inc., in Dewitt, Iowa. He's put in thirty years of "hard time" breaking rocks in the quarry business. He casually switches between driving different types of equipment the way most people switch between using a knife and fork.

Working in a portable quarry operation between Ft. Madison and Burlington, Iowa, Dick Carber spends a good part of his day pushing piles of rocks around with a well-worn Caterpillar D7 equipped with a Carco TD-18 winch manufactured in 1957.

Next page
Perched precariously on the lip of a quarry shelf, this Komatsu-made bulldozer has just finished shoving a load of rocks over the side. Tanker trucks continually spray water, which helps keep down the dust churned up by these machines. A skilled bulldozer operator, ever at risk of going over the lip, hopes never to put his dozer's rollover protection system to the test. A simple lap belt holds him to his seat.

Above
A massive, reinforced bulldozer blade attached to an equally massive machine such as this Komatsu dozer literally moves mountains. Notice that the machine's high-mounted headlights are on; this helps the driver see in the dim light and dusty air of the quarry.

Next page
The Komatsu 575A-2 is the world's largest bulldozer. It weighs 291,010lb and uses a 1050hp V-12 engine to push a giant 70yd-capacity, high-tensile strength, steel U-dozer blade. The operator's cab is mounted on rubber shock absorbers. *Komatsu Dresser Company*

Chapter 8

Farm Hand

Left
Sugar cane is burned before it is harvested. On this plantation, dozer operators plunge into the still-smoldering fields and push the cane into huge piles, which are then loaded by crane into massive trailer trucks for the trip to the crushing plant.

Above
Standing atop an Iowa levee, this huge TD 25c International Harvester weighs in at 96,000lb and uses a 310hp engine to push a massive 18.5ft-long, 5.5ft-tall bulldozer blade. The rear attachment is a hydraulically operated drainage tile plow.

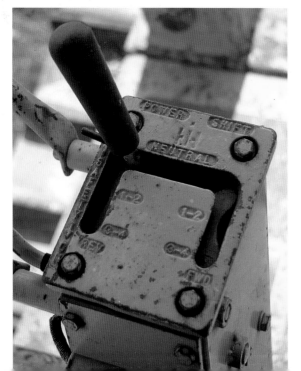

Mike Pieper operates a small fleet of bulldozers from his farm in Weaver, Iowa. He uses this Work Brau tile plow to cut a 17.5in-wide slot for laying plastic water drain tile. To enable the plow to cut to its maximum 8ft depth, Pieper has chained together up to seven vehicles, including two International Harvester TD 25c crawlers and two Caterpillar D8s.

There's plenty of power behind the shift lever of this International Harvester. It slips into its forward and reverse gears when moved into the side slots, and keeps the machine in neutral when positioned up top as shown here.

When the levee in Weaver broke during a driving rainstorm at 1 o'clock in the morning on July 11, 1993, 14,000 acres of prime Iowa farmland went underwater. Two breaks in the 22-mile-long levee surrounding Green Bay Bottom—breaks totaling nearly three-fourths of a mile—allowed the rain-swollen Mississippi to sweep over dozens of farms in less than 48 hours. In the rush to get people and animals to safety, this 10ft-tall Caterpillar D4 was one of the casualties left behind. Even after being submerged for weeks, it may still be salvageable.

Working to rebuild the broken Green Bay Bottom levee surrounding his 3,200-acre farm, Mike Pieper slogs through the thick Mississippi River mud in a Caterpillar D6C equipped with extra lights, a full ROPS, Hyster W6EC winch, and Balderson blade. The dozer's wide track helps spread its weight and keeps it from sinking into soft surfaces such as this mud.

With water over his entire farm, Mike Pieper can't help but get his Cat tractor's feet wet. He put in 18-hour days to build a pumping station he designed to drain the area flooded by the levee breaks.

Like the proverbial postman who can't be stopped by mud, rain, sleet, or snow, this Cat D6C undercarriage delivers under the toughest of conditions.

Previous page
A John Deere 850B Long Track and a Caterpillar D5B take a short rest from round-the-clock work in a Hawaiian sugar cane field. The red soil is a product of Hawaii's volcanic origin.

Above
Equipped with a specialized curved rake with springs, this Cat D5B has been modified to sweep up piles of sugar cane on the island of Kauai.

Next page
Seen from the air, four bulldozers and accompanying scrapers carve out a new vineyard in the rolling hills north of Healdsburg, California. Unequaled in its ability to change the lay of the land, the bulldozer plays an important part in agricultural operations all over the world.

Previous page
Thousands of acres of sugar cane, a crop once harvested by many people and horses, begin the trip to your table, courtesy of one man and his machine.

Down on the farm, if you need it now, you build it. Here, a hitching bracket is welded to the back of a Caterpillar D9 ripper assembly.

Sixty-one-year-old Tom Burger of Yorkville, California, catches a little rest between farm and logging jobs with his old Cat D7 and 1941-vintage Hyster winch. He has driven dozers since he was 12 and has a simple philosophy: "You just get on and run them."

Sometimes field repairs are necessary. In a vineyard outside of Healdsburg, California, the mechanics working on this D9G have it made in the shade.

This Cat D7 has traded its blade for an unusual spaded rake attachment used for plowing down thick stalks of cane. The operator wears a mask to filter out dust and smoke—notice the fire extinguisher—which billows up during the harvesting operation.

What you see is what you get—in this case, a Cat D7. The solid steel specifications plate is as sturdy as the machine. A tin plate like those found on cars would never do on a dozer.

Just outside the little town of Dickson Mounds, Illinois, a John Deere JD 450 gets tucked away at the end of the day in a bed of rolled bales of hay.

Chapter 9

Landfill Load

Left
Pushing a ton of trash before it, a Caterpillar tractor makes room for more at the Sonoma County, California, sanitary landfill. The extra catch-guard extending above the blade keeps trash from rolling over the top and piling up in front of the tractor.

Above
Sanitary landfills are made sanitary by alternating layers of dirt and garbage. This old Cat D9N is used to rip up the soil and push it into piles to be picked up by a scraper.

To get a full load of dirt, rubber-tired scrapers often require a little push from their beefy bulldozer brothers.

Previous page
Seemingly oblivious to the monster machine at work beside it, a neatly camouflaged sea gull scans Sonoma County's rubbish for its next meal. Note the clothing and other garbage caught up amidst the treads. Garbage is on a fast track with this dozer.

More Glamorous Jobs: Dozers in the Movies

Dozens of dozers have had featured parts in movies. Who can forget the classic *Fighting Seabees* with none other than John Wayne playing the part of a heroic dozer driver who, under a hail of sniper bullets, saves the day by driving his dozer into a gas tank to torch attacking tanks? (If you haven't seen it, don't worry. Nobody kills The Duke. It's just a flesh wound.)

Mel Gibson rampaged through a housing tract with bullets bouncing off the blade of his bulldozer in a *Lethal Weapon* flick. It just shows that it doesn't pay to get in the way of a mad Australian road warrior with a loaded dozer.

Some of the other movies featuring dozers: The sci-fi *Tremors* featured Kevin Bacon and Fred Ward rumbling across the desert in a dozer to escape a mutant killer worm—a very big one, of course. *Vanishing Point* ended with a drug-dazed driver running his car straight into a dozer roadblock at about 100mph. The infamous *Killdozer*, filmed in 1974, saw a deadly dozer with a mind of its own try to do in Clint Walker, Robert Urich, and an entire construction crew.

If you can round them up, these movies would make a great night of down and dirty dozer action on your VCR at home.

While it looks like it might be ready for the scrap heap itself, this well-worn Caterpillar D6C is just getting an overhaul. Within a few days, mechanics had it back on the job at the landfill.

Chapter 10

Armored Blades

The Dozer Wages War.

Militarized dozers have seen plenty of action, from Pacific beaches in World War II all the way to the shifting sands of the Saudi Arabian desert during the crises in the Gulf. In war paint, this versatile machine has been called on to level everything from landing strips to land mines. Its role was so key in World War II that legendary tank commander General George Patton once said that if he were forced to choose between using tanks and bulldozers for an invasion, he'd take dozers every time.

Stories of dozer drivers overcoming insurmountable obstacles to achieve their objectives are legendary. Here are just a few of them.

An 88,000lb D8N gets a lift directly from Caterpillar's headquarters in Peoria, Illinois, to Kuwait via a giant C-5A military transport. In the aftermath of the Gulf War, many machines like this were equipped with fire-fighting capabilities and rushed overseas to help put out the oil well fires started by Iraq's retreating army. *Caterpillar, Inc.*

Normandy—Putting a Pillbox out of Action

Faced with withering fire from a German pillbox—a low, concrete bunker filled with machine guns—during the invasion of Normandy, British Royal Engineers trundled a dozer around to a "blind spot" in back of the beach-front fortification. There, they dropped the blade on their dozer and began pushing a mound of earth, angling it into the firing slits cut in the side of the enemy-held machine gun nest. One by one, each slit was smothered, and each gun silenced, opening a bullet-free path for British soldiers to advance up the beach.

Kuwait—Filling a Trench

The Iraqi army that invaded Kuwait dug deeply fortified trenches and awaited the inevitable assault by Allied armored forces. But they didn't count on the ingenuity of US engineers. Avoiding a frontal attack, tanks fitted with earth-moving blades swung parallel to the trench line, one on either side of the enemy. As they held down the entrenched troops with machine gun fire, the tanks lowered their blades and plowed slowly, steadily

In the high desert of the Army's Ft. Irwin National Training Center outside Barstow, California, 19-year-old Specialist Brad Kincaid of Kentucky puts a 19-ton M-9 ACE (Armored Combat Earthmover) from the 1st Cavalry Division, 91st Engineers Battalion, into action. His unit is based in Killeen, Texas. Designed to keep up with the Army's fast tanks and armored troop transports, the unarmed ACE rolls along at a top speed of 37 miles per hour (mph). A 260hp Cummins 903 engine provides the power. Before dozing, the entire vehicle dips at the nose and the ACE's hinged blade opens to scoop up an additional 1.5 ton of dirt in a unique central cavity. The added weight increases traction and the dirt is dumped before travel. The vehicle's one-person crew is protected by a 3/8in-thick armor plate.

ahead, filling the trench with tons of earth and burying any opposition.

"Vera," the Battlefield Bulldozer

Advancing right behind the first wave of infantry, in the face of shrapnel from shells and mortars during an attack on a German-held position during World War II, Corporal J. B. Hillsdon of the Royal Engineers cleverly used his bulldozer's bulk to protect him while he worked. After lowering the blade and setting the controls for slow forward, he and his crewman jumped off their beloved "Vera" (they also called their machine "The Rolling Stone") and huddled behind her as she cut a path for the tanks and armored vehicles to follow, pelted by bullets and bombs. An accompanying infantry officer was so impressed that he inquired if this unmanned bulldozer was actually a robot.

Praised by general and infantry joe alike, the bulldozer has earned a well-deserved reputation as an indispensable piece of military equipment. As one World War II serviceman put it, "They could have sent us all the airplanes in the world, but if they hadn't sent us bulldozers, too, we might as well have stayed home."

If it has to, the ACE can even float across a stream with the addition of a strapped-on rubber collar. The tracks double as paddles.

Although not primarily designed for dozing dirt, the M-88 Recovery Vehicle is fitted with a bulldozer blade for pushing vehicles and debris out of the way. Its main job is towing tanks.

The most heavily armed dirt digger in the U.S. Army's arsenal is the M1A1 tank. Fitted with a mine plow, the tank pushes through the ground at a speed of 8 to 10mph while burrowing up lethal mines. The plow is manually lowered to one of three pre-set depths by a cable controlled by the tank's driver. It is retracted by two electric motors.

There's not much that can stop this tank. In the Gulf War, even direct hits by Iraq's T-72 tanks just bounced off the M1A1's armor.

Gunner Tim Thomas, Vehicle Commander Donald Quinn, Driver Jeffrey DeRosa, and Loader Dwaine Randall crew this CEV (Combat Engineer Vehicle). Here, they take a short break before an after-action review of a training exercise at Ft. Irwin. Capable of defending itself if necessary, this armored dozer carries a 50 caliber M-85 machine gun in the top turret and a 7.62-millimeter (mm) M-240 machine gun in the main turret. It fires a 65lb charge of C4 plastic explosive from its large 165mm demolition gun. The charge bursts upon impact to blow up obstacles the CEV can't push out of the way. Top speed for the 57.5-ton vehicle is about 35mph; it averages 15-20mph in cross-country travel.

To make the training battlefield seem more realistic, Ft. Irwin's 1000sq mi of desert include several well-shot-up wrecks. To clear a path for smaller vehicles during a battle against the base's resident OPFOR (Opposing Force), this CEV uses its blade to push one of these blasted hulks out of the way. The vehicle's boom can lift up to 35,000lb and it can tow nearly 50,000lb.

INDEX